The Advent A

To Alison Norris, who died while this
book was being written, and to Janet Morley:
women of faith, wisdom and integrity.

ACKNOWLEDGEMENTS

Special thanks are due to a number of people who have encouraged
me in writing this book and who in their different ways have con-
tributed to its contents. They include: Brian, Danny, Mick, Stephen
and Gus and other members of the PATH Group, past and present;
Jackie Treetops, Eve Rose, Celia Savage, and Syd Wilkinson who
insisted on lending me a word processor that works. Above all, I
would like to thank Jane for her love, encouragement and clear
thinking. Finally I would like to express my appreciation to SPCK,
and in particular my editor, Alison Barr, for their willingness to
share in this Advent Adventure. After publishing my first book I did
not expect them to give me a second chance.

By the same author:

FAITH IN DARK PLACES

Combining moving stories from the inner city with a fresh
approach to the gospel, *Faith in Dark Places* explores the
revolutionary idea that the good news of God's love is being
spoken to a tired and damaged world by those rejected as
worthless: the homeless and the poor.

'Scenes and encounters from contemporary urban life jostle
with stories retold from the gospels: equally raw and immediate, equally resonant with God.'
Janet Morley

The Advent Adventure

David Rhodes

TRIANGLE

First published in Great Britain in 1998 by
Triangle, SPCK,
Marylebone Road, London NW1 4DU

ACKNOWLEDGEMENTS
Unless otherwise stated, biblical quotations are from
The New English Bible (NEB) copyright © 1961, 1970 Oxford and
Cambridge University Presses. Extracts from the *Revised Standard Version*
(RSV) are copyright © 1971 and 1982.

British Library Cataloguing-in-Publication Data
A catalogue record for this book is available from
the British Library

ISBN 0-281-05159-3

Photoset by Pioneer Associates, Perthshire
Printed in Great Britain by
Caledonian International Ltd, Glasgow

Contents

———

Contents

Introduction

One sunny April morning my mother died. It was a few days after my seventh birthday and it was very sudden. I remember my father breaking the news to me. The next few years were a nightmare, moving from town to town as my father changed jobs again and again. He did his best, but I still remember the dark nights and the rainy streets and the feeling that I did not belong anywhere.

It has been said that one of our most basic instincts is the search for security and meaning. I'm sure that has been true for me – especially influenced by those difficult early years.

Working as a journalist on national newspapers, I found financial security but very little meaning. Later, when I was unexpectedly ordained as an Anglican priest, I found meaning as well, and the meaning became much more important than the security.

Then, a few years ago, it all changed again. When I left the security of the parish ministry to work alongside homeless people in the city it seemed like a return to the dark years of my childhood. Being with people whose own lives were often a nightmare felt a bit too close for comfort. But I took a deep breath and stepped out boldly. And fell flat on my face.

Instead of taking the gospel to 'the poor' as I fondly imagined, I found the homeless people I encountered were bringing the gospel to me. Whether or not I was sharing the love of God with them, they were certainly sharing it with me.

I realize now that it was only when I plucked up the courage to leave the security of the parish that I began to discover the reality of faith. Before that I had read the gospel. Now it was as though it was being lived out, and I was caught up in that process. It was like being on the inside of what God was doing.

Suddenly, there seemed to be a deeper meaning to faith as life in the city reflected an unexpected significance back into the gospel, the gospel I had taken for granted for so many years. Suddenly the familiar became unfamiliar – even exciting.

It's not all moonlight and roses, of course. Many if not all of the thousands of homeless people in Britain experience great suffering. Whether through the sheer hardship of their existence, their mental or physical illness, depression, feelings of guilt, or through acts of violence, they are in pain. The biggest single cause of death among homeless people sleeping rough is suicide. And people commit suicide because they are in despair.

Winter is the worst time of year, and Christmas, which should stand as a beacon of hope, can be particularly hard. This festival is probably celebrated by more people in Britain than any other, although whether we are worshipping the God of Jesus Christ or Mammon, the god of greed, is another matter.

But what does Christmas mean, this time of year when people suddenly expect to be drawn together in love and harmony with Santa and snowflakes and Bing Crosby and office parties, but instead wake up with expensive hang-overs? We try to buy the security – and find we have lost the meaning.

What does Christmas mean to the people thrown on the economic scrap-heap? People who slip from unemployment into despair and sometimes into homelessness? For many there seems to be no meaning.

The bitter irony is that Christmas – the Christ birth – was for them. What we celebrate is the profound and disturbing work of God in the birth of the one who came to bring good news to the poor. That means the real poor: the destitute. The word 'poor' in Luke's gospel, where we find the Christmas story, means 'beggar'. Not humble and meek and mild; not the sanitized 'poor in spirit', but the real poor.

Suddenly we are confronted by this collision of images. The commercial Christmas of crowded shops, where my homeless friends are not welcome, is confronted by the image of the Christ-child, the stable and the cross. What does it mean?

In our own search for security we will find ourselves drawn to the comfort of the crowded shops and the ringing tills. But if we want to find meaning, we would do better to stick with our friends on the streets, and our friend the Christ person. It will not be comfortable, but it will be real. And in that reality there will be a deeper security: the security of being held in God's love.

That's what this book is about: the search for meaning. It is a journey through the weeks of Advent, which lead up to Christmas, and through into the new year. Each day we try to explore something of the meaning of what God is doing, listening to his word and seeing how that word makes sense in our own streets and cities.

At first it seems a simple matter: gently unwrapping the Christmas story in a quiet process of reflection on the meaning of Advent and the birth of Christ. But gradually all sorts of other things start happening as the implications of God's love begin to spill out.

So be warned: if you love security and comfort, this book will probably disturb you. If you love organized religion, it is sure to infuriate you. But if you want to find meaning and the love of God, then come with us on this Advent adventure.

1 DECEMBER

The adventure begins

In the city centre the wet streets glitter with the reflection of the Christmas lights and the shops blaze with colour in the darkening winter afternoons. The Christmas lights have been up for weeks and the streets are full of shoppers, all seemingly driven by the unspoken anxiety that they may not be ready for the big event.

This year's essential gift is a children's electronic game retailing at £200: more than twice what some people earn in a week. Regardless of family income, every child must have one. It will be all round the playground if they do not. Ironically, the poorest families spend large amounts on expensive children's presents in a desperate attempt to be the same as other people. Christmas can be a very competitive time of year.

Meanwhile, the supermarkets brace themselves for the coming rush for food and drink. Some will remain open 24 hours a day to meet the demand. It is essential to lay in adequate supplies; we are talking about survival here. The shops will all be closed on Christmas Day, and some on Boxing Day as well.

The freedom to spend is one of our most cherished civil liberties and, increasingly, a psychological necessity. Deprived of that freedom for even a few hours, people react in interesting ways. A church group taking part in a poverty awareness exercise were cast adrift alone in the city centre for a day. They were each allowed to take with them only 50p to spend on food. Cheque-books and credit cards were left behind.

The event was designed to give these middle-class churchgoers a glimpse of what it might be like to have fewer

1

choices than normal, and to help them reflect on the way we order society. Leaving the base camp of a city-centre church, they went their separate ways, returning eight hours and two mealtimes later to share their stories.

One person said that after only four hours they had experienced significant emotional distress, and others commented on the feelings of exclusion and detachment. Despite the fact that they knew the situation was only temporary, and the exercise was one they had chosen to take part in, they had still felt a strong sense of alienation.

'I felt I didn't belong. I was on the edge. It was as though I wasn't there,' commented one participant. 'It made me realize how much having money and the freedom to spend it makes me feel part of society. It was an alarming discovery.'

But out in that same city centre today, most people are well equipped with cheque-books and credit cards. 'If you've got it, spend it' is the law of the High Street. And if you haven't got it, you can still spend it. There is interest-free credit and all the time in the world to pay. The shops are warm and inviting and the piped Christmas music soothes our frayed nerves. Shopping has become a major leisure activity.

Only the Church seems not to have caught on to the fact that Christmas is coming. Two days ago we changed, not to the white and gold of joyful celebration, but to the sombre purple vestments of the season of Advent. What was all that about?

The High Street retailers rush in where angels fear to tread. But, for once, the Church has not been left behind. Like an athlete pausing to focus, concentrating on the leap ahead, so we too pause to focus on the unfolding significance of Christmas.

But what is the significance of Christmas? And what does this little-known season of Advent mean? Why do we bother with any of this when all we need to do is to go with the crowd? Are we part of the crowd? And, if not, who are we?

Suddenly we find ourselves stumbling over the enormous question: who am I?

As the people taking part in that awareness exercise discovered, the important thing about shopping is that it gives us comfort. Adding to our already considerable possessions, we feel even more secure. Our world is increasingly filled with what we own and what we can control. We are protected by a wall of wealth from such unsettling issues.

Now, with unfashionable integrity, the Church lays before us a time to reflect on who we are and what we are called to be.

'Advent' is the beginning of the word 'adventure', and faith is an adventure or it is nothing. It is a journey into the unknown: leaving the secure and comfortable behind and moving into unfamiliar territory. A time to ask questions.

As with many journeys, we will encounter other travellers on the way. Who will they be and where do they come from? And is this a real journey? Or is it a sentimental Nativity play for grown-ups?

'Christmas? Humbug!' shouted Scrooge. He had better things to do than keep a ridiculous religious festival. There was business to be done and profits to be made.

But, suddenly, his secure little world falls apart: in three terrifying dreams the ghosts of Christmas – past, present and future – reveal other possibilities to him. His dreams are not real, but they speak to him of reality. He does not want to make that journey, but finds himself unwillingly in a new place. He has been led out of darkness into light.

Our journey is not one of dreams, but it is one which involves names and situations so familiar and so much associated with childhood that, to the adult mind, they may seem unreal. And they are set in an age so far from ours that, again, there is a sense of unreality. Can we, as mature adults, be seriously thinking of doing business with three wise men, angels and a stable?

We need to ask at the outset whether we are willing to make this journey and run the risk of wasting valuable time, or whether we are too grown-up for all this and, with Scrooge, turn away with a shout of 'Humbug!'

Was there really a star, or was it all a dream? Dazzled by

the bright lights of the shopping-centre streets, we may not at first notice the smaller light. The night sky in winter is more often than not obscured by cloud. Ironically, Christmas may be exactly the wrong time of year to try to glimpse a star.

2 DECEMBER

Ground zero

---◆---

The industrial West Riding of Yorkshire is not the most beautiful part of God's creation, especially on a foggy winter afternoon.

In the bad old days before the clean-air regulations were introduced, the valleys were often choked with smog. Driving over the hills, you could look down on what appeared to be a lake of pollution with the mill chimneys sticking up through the fog into the clean air and belching more smoke into the atmosphere.

But out of this world of fine worsted cloth, millstone grit and industrial filth, there came each Christmas the most wonderful sound. It was, and still is, the Huddersfield Choral Society singing Handel's oratorio, *Messiah*.

Whether you are religious or not, the sound of a hundred voices singing the 'Hallelujah Chorus' takes some beating. For once in the year the town's pretentious and rather threadbare town hall seems to come into its own and something profoundly wonderful happens.

To the outsider there is something quite unexpected about some of the finest music in the world coming out of this very ordinary industrial town.

But, just as the majestic and overwhelming music of Handel's *Messiah* seems somehow out of place in a town like Huddersfield, so too the Advent story begins with an apparently inappropriate situation. If Advent is a time for reflection on the story of Christmas, then what does it mean and where does it begin?

Somebody once wrote that Jesus was a northerner. It comes as something of a shock to realize that story of the

Prince of Peace, about whom the *Messiah* was written, begins not in a great and sophisticated city like Rome or Paris or Vienna, but in a place like Huddersfield.

And, according to the surviving accounts, this momentous event involved not princes and palaces but a young peasant woman. Had she lived in Huddersfield, she might have been a young mill girl. Two thousand years of tradition and theology have elevated this young woman to the heights of religious adoration and esteem. But the Advent story begins long before all that. And, as with many of the things of God, it begins at ground zero – with absolutely nothing.

There is a bizarre contrast between the magnitude of the event and the way it all comes about.

St John, who had had a lot of time to think things over, writes in the opening verses of his gospel: 'In the beginning was the Word . . . and the Word was with God, and the Word was God. . . . And the Word became flesh and dwelt among us' and later: 'God so loved the world that he gave his own beloved son' (John 1:1, 14; 3:16, RSV).

Writing probably 70 or 80 years after the events we are exploring, what is this deep-thinking disciple saying? Nothing less than that the Word of God, the creative expression of the God of all the universe, was being born into the world as a human being.

The words of St John are every bit as majestic and as powerful as the words and music of Handel's *Messiah*, but the context of this event is far more unexpected than the town hall in Ramsden Street, Huddersfield.

It is not to a professor of theology or to an archbishop that the Word comes: it is not to a princess in a palace who is caught up in this drama and placed at the centre of this momentous event. It is a complete nobody.

The insignificant Mary carries the Word of God in her womb just as, years later, another insignificant woman, called Mary Magdalene, was to carry the equally astonishing news of resurrection to the disbelieving disciples. She, too, was a nobody.

Two obscure and unimportant women caught up in the work of God, while the rich, the clever, the powerful and the religious are left aside. Neither of these women, as far as we know, had any particular involvement in the religious power structures of their day. Neither appears to have been particularly well educated; and neither seems to have had any great social standing.

Indeed, as women, they had minimal social status anyway. Remember the words of the religious men who prayed each day in thanksgiving that they had not been born a Gentile or a woman.

What time and tradition have made normal and acceptable, common sense shows to be ridiculous and unlikely. Is this really how God would choose to work when such important matters are in hand?

Judging by the rest of the gospels, and much of the Old Testament, we realize the answer to that question is an unexpected yes.

Was it not out of slavery in Egypt that the Jewish community was born, a people without power – even without freedom? Were they not created as the most significant community of faith in the world, out of absolutely nothing?

And then we remember that we are talking here about creation. It is out of nothing that God brings life and hope and purpose.

Take another well-known example. Who was one of the most important people in the unfolding history of that faith community? King David. But where did he come from?

According to the records, the attempt to select a new king had ground to an embarrassing and confusing halt. Finally David is located, dirty and untidy, looking after the family's flocks of sheep. Not exactly Eton and Cambridge. Not, at first sight, officer material. How many people have made the step from agricultural labourer to king in one easy move?

But God resolutely pushes ahead with his task of creation: bringing life to the world. And this rank-smelling nobody from the sheep-folds does become king.

But are these not just isolated incidents? Hardly. When we

look more closely we see that the source documents of our faith are littered with examples of God choosing the weak and the powerless to be at the centre of this majestic process of creation. A process into which we may find ourselves being drawn.

The Advent adventure begins with a peasant girl and an angel. Peasant girls we can at least visualize. But what are we to make of angels?

3 DECEMBER

Inner-city angel

———◆———

Angels may have been two a penny two thousand years ago, but they are not so common now. Isn't it rather odd that Luke can simply say: 'The angel Gabriel was sent by God with a message for a girl called Mary' (Luke 1:26–7), with no apparent need to explain what the word 'angel' meant?

Was belief in angels as messengers of God so widespread that this could pass without comment from the gospel writer, other than to say which particular angel it was?

It is strange to think that something which appears to have been an acceptable and recognizable event in Luke's day is a mysterious and perplexing question in ours. What is an angel? Is there such a thing? Was there such a thing? And what was going on in that encounter?

Perhaps the first thing to realize is that God makes the first move. And that, we should remember, is a crucial thread running through the whole of our faith experience. God takes the initiative.

Second, whether or not angels were commonplace in the ancient world, this one seems to have given the young girl a profound shock. According to Luke, Mary is not suddenly filled with joy. Instead, she feels fear. So much so that she has to be reassured with the words 'Do not be afraid. God has been gracious to you.' And this graciousness involves gift, not threat.

Third, whether or not we know what angels are, or whether we believe they exist, it seems clear that this young woman was convinced that something important was happening.

What she believed was happening was an event involving

9

power and authority. The angel was a messenger from God: 'The Holy Spirit will come upon you. You shall bear a son and his name will be Jesus. God will give him the throne of his ancestor, David, and he will be king over Israel for ever. His reign will never end' (Luke 1:35, 30–33).

And Mary replied: 'I am the Lord's servant. As you have spoken, so be it' (1:38).

Once again the tradition of centuries has washed away the rough edges of our credulity – or, for many people, created sandbanks of cynicism and disbelief. These few short sentences from Luke's gospel raise more questions than we can answer in a lifetime, especially as much of the material is locked into a different cultural world.

But, despite the differences in culture, one basic question needs to be answered if we are to continue our journey through Advent. And the question is this: does God speak to people? Not: are there characters in white smocks with wings and harps? but: does God speak to people like you and me, here and now?

The following story may provide part of the answer.

Some time ago a priest working with homeless people found himself at a pretty low ebb. He had been working too hard and had made a number of mistakes. They were not matters of life and death, but they were enough to dent his self-confidence.

Not having a church of his own, he often helped out when other clergy were ill or on holiday. But this particular weekend he was free of any duty. Feeling depressed and incompetent, he knew he needed help. But where does a fed-up priest go for help? When Sunday came he went to a neighbouring church and tucked himself away in the back row.

By chance a homeless man he knew came into the church and sat down beside him. During the service they exchanged a few quiet words, but the priest was not really paying much attention. He was thinking about his own problems.

Meanwhile, the service rolled on. Suddenly he found they were at the point just before the sharing of the bread and the wine. In this particular service the congregation says together: 'Lord, I am not worthy to receive you, but only say the word and I shall be healed.'

For the priest huddled away in the back row of the church that day, the words seemed like a great hurdle to be jumped. Never had they had more meaning. And so when the moment came he must have spoken them with particular feeling.

The memory, not only of his recent mistakes, but of a lifetime of failings and errors seemed to come flooding back as he said: 'only say the word and I shall be healed.'

As he uttered the words in what was for him a fervent but impossible prayer, it seemed as though there was an instant of complete silence. Then a quiet voice at his side said in a warm Irish accent: 'Sure, you're not so bad, my friend.'

The priest did not know whether to laugh or cry, but he felt a great weight lifted from him. It felt like healing. It was certainly one of the most vivid and memorable moments of his life. They were words which were true and which he would never forget. The next time he made a mistake, perhaps he would hear that voice saying, not that he was perfect, but 'you're not so bad, my friend.'

Does God speak to people? The priest had gone into that church in need of healing and reassurance. He needed to hear the word of God spoken to him. 'Only say the word, and I shall be healed,' he had prayed.

And the word had been spoken: directly, firmly and lovingly. The sacrament of healing and absolution had come from a homeless man who was neither priest nor angel. But perhaps, at that moment, was both.

Do we really expect angels to have wings and to be dressed in white? What if they sometimes wear old clothes and smell of stale beer and tobacco? At that moment was that homeless man not speaking the word of God?

Perhaps – at that precise moment. But how strange that this is almost identical to the phrase used to describe the way God loves us: 'the sacrament of the present moment'. It is the realization that we are being loved by God, totally, specially and individually, at this precise and present moment of existence. At the moment one person types in these words on a word processor; at the moment another person reads these words off the page.

The sacrament of the present moment says that *now* is the God-given and God-blessed special time. It is a healthy counterbalance to the tendency a lot of us have to live our lives in the past, imprisoned by nostalgia – or regret.

Similarly, the sacrament of the present moment guards against living in a fantasy world of tomorrows. God is loving us now and calling us into life now – not at some time in the far-distant future. Pie in the sky when you die is not what the gospel is about. The gospel is about loving God and our neighbour now: in the sacrament and reality of the present moment.

It means that true spirituality is inseparable from politics and economics, and real prayer is inseparable from social justice. Why? Because the sacrament of the present moment is about love, and love cannot be compartmentalized.

But this doesn't seem to fit too well with our traditional idea of Christmas. It doesn't seem to fit with Christmas-card images of church bells across the snow and carols from King's College, Cambridge.

But maybe it does fit with the Christ-child born in a cattle shed to an unmarried mother, and with a man dying naked on a cross. Both of those events were real moments in real life, and both were profoundly sacraments of the present moment: God truly and overwhelmingly loving the world in both of those events; God truly and overwhelmingly loving that battered and confused priest at the back of a city church.

4 DECEMBER

Strange encounter

---◆---

It is one of the frustrations of life that, looking back, we can often see a clear path that we have taken over the years. We can see how events have fitted together in a way that seems to have given direction and purpose to our lives. Like the wake of a ship through the water, there is a clear line.

The problem is that we do not always see with the same degree of clarity when we look ahead into the future. The path ahead often seems indistinct and we feel we are faced with a maze of possibilities. We may well try to live the sacrament of the present moment, but we are sailing into uncharted waters and we are, after all, only human.

When should we say yes to something and when should we say no? What is it that God is calling us to do in this present moment? And is it God, or is it just our own imaginings?

Reading those first few pages of Luke's gospel, it all seems to be so clear and straightforward. But in reality it was probably neither. We get a hint of that when Luke says that Mary was 'deeply troubled and wondered what the greeting might mean' (Luke 1:29).

We know from the parallel account in the gospel of Matthew that Joseph, Mary's husband-to-be, was also thoroughly confused about what was going on. His first instinct was to set aside their formal and binding engagement in what would have amounted to an act of divorce. A serious move.

These were not two superhuman and saintly figures serenely bowing to the will of God. They were two ordinary people struggling to make sense of an unexpected and alarming situation which neither of them had sought.

The great tennis-player Billie Jean King once said that champions are people who keep trying till they get it right. Saints are ordinary people who keep struggling with the Word of God until they get it as right as they can in one lifetime.

Mary seems to have got it right, but not without a struggle. And maybe there were two key factors that helped her: first, she was willing to trust God and, second, she was able to talk it over with a friend. And both are vitally important for us if we want to make sense of God's Word.

First, then, Mary trusted God. But what sort of God? A ruthless and autocratic tyrant, ruling the universe from afar? No, Mary trusted a God of love and gentle courtesy. If there was an angel, why was there an angel? Why did God bother to tell this unimportant peasant girl what was going on? Why not simply let the child be born and let the mother remain in ignorance of what was happening? What difference would it have made?

The answer seems to be that God is not like that. Look what happens in that strange encounter. It begins with a courteous greeting expressed with humility and deference, the young woman being addressed as 'most favoured one', and an assurance of well-being: 'the Lord is with you'.

The encounter is about a gift. Mary will be blessed with the birth of a son. Not only that, he will be the greatest king that her nation has ever known, greater even than King David: 'His reign will never end' (Luke 1:34).

Then there is a pause. And in that moment the young woman has the opportunity to refuse to co-operate. She can say no to God – as we all can. Years later St John was to describe the Christ person as saying: 'I stand at the door and knock.' If we decide to open the door, he will come in, but he will not kick the door down. There is the same courtesy and humility here. God knocks at the door and waits for the young peasant girl to say yes.

Mary's assent is implicit in her bemused reply: 'But how

can this happen?' The nature of the reply indicates that she knows the child will not be her husband's, although that would have been by far the most obvious assumption to make.

Suddenly the mood of the encounter changes gear as the full implications of the situation are revealed. A profound act of creation is then foretold: the power of the Holy Spirit will overshadow her.

But what is this Holy Spirit? Nothing less than the awesome and dynamic spirit of God we see hovering over the waters of chaos in the primal event of creation in the Book of Genesis.

What will she say to this frightening new possibility that has opened up before her? Will she say yes – and allow the awesome creative power of God to enter her life? Or will she run away, preferring peace and quiet?

Again, it is as if there is a moment of deep silence. Then Mary responds with words which go to the heart both of prayer and Christian discipleship. Having been silent and attentive before God, she has made space to hear the word of life. The word is awesome in its power and implications. But her response is simple: 'I am the Lord's servant. As you have spoken, so be it.' Mary is saying: 'I trust you. You are at the centre and I will walk with you.'

The angel leaves her and the encounter is, for the moment, at an end. But a second profound act of creation is already taking place. It concerns her older cousin, Elizabeth, to whom Mary now hurries to share her own story.

Hidden meanings

Sometimes you need to be a bit of a detective to read the Bible. Stories which, on the face of it, are simple and straight-forward sometimes turn out to have a deeper meaning. That's what happens next.

Mary is told, not only that she is to have a child, but that her cousin or kinswoman, Elizabeth, is also to have a baby. At first that sounds simple enough, except that such an event is impossible. Elizabeth is old – long past child-bearing age. There is no chance of her having a child at her time of life.

Not only that, she has been barren all her life. The full force of this situation is lost to us now, but if there was one thing worse than being born a woman in her culture, it was being a woman who could not have children.

In those days children were believed to be a sign of God's favour and blessing. To be infertile was thought to be a sure sign of God's displeasure. All her adult life Elizabeth had lived with this shame and humiliation. But something strange is going on here. Both Elizabeth and her husband are described as being very devout people who had lived blamelessly according to the ordinances and commands of God. So how can they be punished by God, if they are blameless?

Maybe something else is being hinted at here. The community of faith in which Elizabeth and her husband Zechariah live was very keen to obey the law of God in every detail. But something was missing; otherwise why did the angel appear to Mary to announce the birth of the saviour, the Messiah? It was assumed that the Messiah was going to 'save' the nation in a political and military sense, so they were on the look-out for a great leader to appear, perhaps some-one like Alexander the Great.

But maybe God had other ideas about what 'saving' the nation meant. Maybe it was more about restoring or creating life-giving relationships of openness and love and trust.

Can it be that the story of the blameless and religiously obedient Elizabeth and her husband is a parable about the nation? Does it indicate that the rigorous religious system to which they were so loyal was also barren? And if this is so, are we now hearing the first condemnation of the sterile religious system into which the Christ person was to come into conflict in later years? A system he was to accuse of being clean and white on the outside like a painted tomb, but full of corruption on the inside? There are some deep resonances here.

But any idea of condemnation is tempered by a second thread which now enters our story: the old woman is to have a child but, contrary to family tradition, he will be called John. Who cares what he is called? Why does this matter?

It matters because the name John means 'gift from God' and it is crucially important that we register that fact. The well-behaved religious couple are not being rewarded for obeying all the rules and regulations: they have not earned this child. The birth is a gift. The first event in Luke's gospel is about God's power expressed in freely given love.

Presented with such an amazing gift, we might expect Elizabeth to be full of joy. But, instead, as soon as she realizes she is going to have a child, she hides herself away for five long months. Why was that?

Think about what has happened. After all these years, she now believes she is pregnant. But what will people think? Is she really pregnant or is she dreaming? Is it a phantom pregnancy? Will she lose the baby? What if she tells everyone what is happening, and then loses the child? Her despair will be even more terrible than it has been in the long barren years, and she will be justly ridiculed for claiming the impossible. So, wisely perhaps, Elizabeth hides herself away – until the day that Mary arrives with her own news.

Mary rushes in and, when Elizabeth hears what she has to say, two things happen simultaneously. First, her own baby kicks in the womb. In that instant there is absolutely no doubt that her own child does exist and is very much alive. For the first time she can allow herself to believe that it is all real, and she reacts with the joy she has kept bottled up for months.

But in the moment that the baby kicks, Elizabeth remembers the promise made to her husband by God. Some translations say that her baby, who is to become John the Baptist, will be filled with the Holy Spirit from the moment of his birth, but the text actually says 'from his mother's womb', meaning that from the moment of conception this child has been part of the unfolding process of God's love.

We are talking here about a present reality, not something that will happen in the future when the baby is eventually born. That present reality is important: Elizabeth cries out in joy, not simply because she knows now that she is pregnant, but because she knows now that she is filled with the Holy Spirit and is being swept along by the power of God.

But why should Mary's arrival have this effect? Perhaps because in the moment that Elizabeth realizes the significance of her own child, she also realizes the significance of what is happening to her young cousin, Mary. Her outburst of joy and exultation suddenly encompasses Mary as well.

The two share their stories. It is as though the two events are ratified. Neither exists in isolation. The one affirms the other.

And this is crucial to our own faith journey. We need to tell our stories to each other, to let the other person hear and reflect on what we are saying. Why? Because things which may seem real and obvious to us may in fact be a trick of the light, a daydream. That is one reason for there being the

Church. It is a community of faith in which together we may try to discern the will of God; not in the privacy of our own thoughts and desires, but in shared reflection among our fellow companions on the journey of faith.

Jesus said: 'I am the truth'. But we need to take time and care to discern what that truth is, to tease out the real from the imagined. Our Advent adventure is not a matter of trying to be religious at Christmas-time, but of trying to discern what is true and meaningful in life. And we need to do that in company with other people.

6 DECEMBER

Out in the cold

The last two days have spoken to us of hope and promise, but today is a day of pain. Not my pain, but other people's. But maybe, because of that, mine too.

Caught up in the tide of shoppers, I had not noticed the man selling newspapers. Gaunt and thin, he stood silently in the windswept shopping precinct, ignored by the passing crowds. From time to time and without warning he uttered the newspaper-seller's harsh cry. It could have been Norwegian for all I could make of it. It sounded like a cry of pain. After each unintelligible shout he reverted to expressionless and introverted silence. Very occasionally someone stopped to buy a paper, but there was no conversation, no change of expression – no human contact.

At his side was a small boy in a padded jacket several sizes too big for him. He squatted quietly on the pavement with his back against the wall. His coat was pulled over his head and his hands were lost in the long sleeves. He must have been seven, perhaps eight, years old.

Across the paved shopping precinct a homeless young woman stood selling *The Big Issue* magazine. She looked pale and underfed. Her hair, plaited in those fashionable dreadlocks, looked unwashed and uncared-for.

Unlike the newspaper-vendor, she spoke to everyone who walked past: '*Big Issue*. Help the homeless. Buy *The Big Issue*.' The crowds seemed to buffet her as they pushed past, avoiding eye contact. But, like a pebble on a beach washed by the surf, she remained at her place, standing first on one foot and then on the other because of the cold.

At her side on a small blanket, a dog dozed. Occasionally

20

it would look up if someone stopped to buy a magazine. From time to time the young woman would roll a cigarette and stoop to pat the dog. It licked her hand with calm familiarity.

Across the way, like a mirror image, the little boy stood up and pulled the coat back off his head. He came quietly to the side of the red metal stall where the man stood selling newspapers. The boy said something, but the man appeared not to hear and did not answer. He did not look down. The boy stood for a moment in silence and then turned away again. There was no contact.

A church clock struck twelve.

I stood for more than 20 minutes wondering who these people were. But I was feeling cold and it was time for me to move on. I had things to do.

Later that day I found myself walking through the shopping precinct again. They were still there. I looked at my watch: two thirty. The little boy had a toy car which he absent-mindedly ran along the pavement at his side. He seemed lost in thought.

There was a wet stain on the pavement like beer from the night before. Or maybe urine. It started to rain, a fine drizzle which made the wind feel even colder. Across the way, the young woman put her magazines in a plastic sleeve to stop them getting wet. Someone else stopped to buy one; always it seemed to be women or young people. They chatted and paused to pat the dog.

That was the difference: across the street no one spoke to the child. At least the dog knew that it was loved.

By five thirty it was dark. They would all be gone by now, but I walked back anyway. Sure enough, the young woman and her dog had gone, but the man and the boy were still there. This time his cry was different, but it seemed that was all that had changed.

For more than half an hour I stood, watching from a distance. The little boy, still silent, seemed unconcerned about the cold and the boredom. What was going on in that young head? Where was his mother?

Shop assistants in blouses and shirt-sleeves, glowing from the day's work, emerged briefly to put out boxes of rubbish. A street-cleaner in fluorescent waterproof jacket began emptying litter bins, his humble work echoing another's servanthood as he quietly washed the feet of the great city. But the newspaper-seller stood unmoved and the boy still waited.

Suddenly, at five past six, another man arrived. There was a conversation and the news-stand was put away. At last it was time to go home – for all of us.

In the city centre the traffic was heavy and the headlights dazzled in the darkness. The two men walked along the shopping precinct and crossed the busy road. They did not glance at the boy wandering along behind them. They crossed another road and I lost them in the crowd.

I thought of another little boy. Other dark nights. Another age.

What do those angel stories we call the Annunciation have to do with them? What does it mean that we are all called out of darkness? What does the promise of yesterday have to do with the girl and her dog, or with the man and the little boy?

On how many street corners and in how many cities had that same scene been played out? And for what? The church clock struck the hours, but where was God in this? And the hope of Christmas?

The Christ-child still to be born was there in that city street, his coat pulled over his head against the cold. Hour after hour, waiting without complaint at the side of a lonely man selling newspapers.

And was God there that day? Yes, he too was on the street. Looking over my shoulder, maybe. Reminding me that these also are his children and that he suffers with them in the cold and the drizzle; in a cattle shed and on a cross.

But what I do about it, I do not know. Except, perhaps, not forget.

7 DECEMBER
Let them eat cake

-------◆-------

The day got off to a bad start: listening to what they call on the radio a programme of news and comment. Someone has had a great idea. Instead of giving money to people who are begging on the city streets, they will hand out luncheon vouchers.

That way these people will not spend our money on booze and fags: they will spend it on food. The hungry will be fed, our consciences will be eased and the problem will be solved. Really?

We have a friend who is on heroin. She takes the drug each day. We do not try to break her of the habit. Why not? Because she is in the advanced stages of terminal cancer. The drug is carefully regulated by the medical staff at the nearby hospice.

If she did not take the drug, under the medical name of morphine, she would be overwhelmed with the pain. The drug, which has no doubt become addictive by now, is essential. It is the only way she can live life and stay sane.

We also have another dear friend who is alcohol-dependent. He takes this drug each day and we do not try to break him of his habit, either. Why not? Because he too is suffering.

He is suffering the multiple effects of both physical and mental illness, which render him incapable of work. He is suffering from political policies which effectively remove from him any chance of living in a warm, secure home. He is suffering from social prejudices which isolate him and from a sense of personal failure which crushes his spirit.

He is a person of sensitivity, wisdom, humour, compassion and love. Occasionally he slips into the back of a church. He is heroic in the way that he faces the multiple problems of life. Often he goes for weeks without a drink, but then the pain starts again. If he did not drink he would be overwhelmed with pain. His drug, heavily advertised and freely available at every supermarket and off-licence in the country, is the only way he can cope with life as he is forced to live it.

To take the drug away from either of these people and offer them a plate of sandwiches instead would not be a very loving or intelligent gesture.

What does it mean to offer homeless people luncheon vouchers? It means that we believe we know what is best for them; it says we think they haven't got the wit to buy a sandwich or a meat pie when they are hungry; it means that we are either unable or unwilling to inquire about their real needs; and it may suggest that our real concern is not their well-being, but that they should not waste the small change we may hand out to them on the street corner.

This Christmas many of us will spend hundreds of pounds on presents and on food and drink with hardly a thought about our January credit-card bill. Yet we will be meticulously judgemental about how a person begging on the street will spend the 20 pence we drop into their hat.

Perhaps they will spend it on cigarettes. So what? How often have I wasted the gifts that God has given me? Not 20 pence that he had dropped into my hat, but the priceless gift of life and creation. After 54 years on this earth, have I really used that gift so well?

Enjoying the material benefits of living in the richest segment of this planet when there is more wealth and comfort possible than at any time in human history, we turn a blind eye to the millions dying of hunger on our television screens and take to task with Victorian thoroughness those who are homeless in our own country.

And what must God be thinking about this nightmare of poverty, plenty and pollution? What must he be thinking about his gift to the world of his own Christ-child? And of the way we receive or reject that gift?

'God so loved the world, that he gave his only son . . .'

The words read out on Christmas morning sound so serene and calming. They might even sound sad, as though God was in quiet despair over the state of the world.

But what if God isn't feeling serene? What if God is feeling very angry about things? Do we catch an echo here of a story that the Christ person himself was to tell, years later?

A landowner left his estate in the hands of his tenants and went away on a long journey. Some time later he sent a servant to collect from the tenants his share of the produce. But the tenants beat the servant and sent him away empty-handed. The landowner sent a second servant, but the tenants thrashed him and treated him outrageously. He tried again, sending a third servant, but he too, was wounded and flung out.

Finally he sent his own son. They will respect him, he thought. But instead the tenants said: 'This is the heir to the estate. Let us kill him, so that the property will come to us.' So they took him out and killed him.

'What will the owner of the estate do to those wicked tenants?' Christ asks. 'He will put them to death and let out the estate to other tenants' (Luke 20:9–16).

Is it stretching the imagination too far to see the parallel between that gospel story and the world today? Between the wicked tenants in control of the estate but abusing their authority and the people who are in positions of political and economic power in the world today? And where is Jesus in this? Perhaps alongside the beggar on our city streets.

'When I was hungry, you gave me no food. When I was naked, you did not clothe me,' he told them (Matthew 25:42–3).

Many of us have been brought up to think that the wrath of God is something that the Victorians invented to keep the lid on sexual freedom and moral misbehaviour. We seldom seem to link the wrath of God with social justice and human oppression. The wrath of God seems to have been hijacked by Christian groups who believe that faith is a privatized one-to-one relationship with God and that sin is largely to do with sexuality.

But faith is social and corporate as well as personal, because human beings are social and corporate creatures. And consequently sin is a social and corporate matter, involving not only personal relationships but also systems of power: politics and economics.

A glance at the Old Testament reading for Evening Prayer on the Second Sunday in Advent gives us a flavour of what this might mean: 'Listen to this, says the Lord God, you who grind the destitute and plunder the humble. You who say, When will the Sabbath be over so that we may open our wheat again . . . tilting the scales fraudulently that we may buy the poor for silver and the destitute for a pair of shoes?' (Amos 8:4–8).

Not exactly the sort of language we might expect to find on a Christmas card.

8 DECEMBER

Solving the mystery

———◆———

It took me some time to discover that the Church has unwritten rules. One of them is: 'Thou shalt not be happy. Joyful, thou mayest be, but remember: joy is no laughing matter.'

I realized this when the General Synod of the Church of England was debating a report called 'The Mystery of Salvation'. All of one summer's afternoon some of the best brains in the Church gnawed on this learned document like a dog with a bone.

Outside, the sun was shining but, inside, things were different. Five hundred Christians were exploring nothing less than the gift of life. But never once was there a hint that we should enjoy exploring this astounding gift from God.

There were no balloons or party hats; not a hint of celebration. It was like a conference of undertakers discussing the price of embalming fluid.

My pal Peter Stoodley was furious about the title of the report: 'Salvation is not a mystery,' he said. And he was right. The Church may sometimes wish that salvation was a mystery, and it may sometimes try to turn it into a mystery. But it isn't.

Salvation is life, and life is as obvious as the flower on the stalk or the softness of a baby's bottom.

Amazingly, we may be able to pin-point the exact moment when salvation stopped being a mystery. And, by chance, it comes as we take the next step in our Advent adventure.

With the help of the gospel of Luke we have started to trace the story of how the Christ-child came to be born. We have seen how Mary is confronted by what she believes to be an angel, and the whole purpose of her life opens up before her. She hurries off to see her cousin, Elizabeth, and their conversation seems to confirm and endorse what Mary is thinking.

Then it is as though there is a pause, during which the full implication of what is happening finally dawns on her. So far there has been fear, confusion, faith and obedience. But until now there has been not a hint of laughter, or celebration.

Now, quite suddenly, it is as though all this wells up in her heart. Perhaps remembering the song of Hannah from the Old Testament, she repeats those immortal words that we know as the Magnificat:

> My soul magnifies the Lord
> and my spirit rejoices in God my saviour.
> For he has regarded the lowliness of
> his handmaiden. For, behold, from henceforth
> all generations shall call me blessed.
> For he that is mighty has magnified me:
> and holy is his name . . .
>
> (Luke 1:46–9)

This great song of praise is important to us for three reasons. First, it is a prayer of thanksgiving which acknowledges a gift. 'God has done all this,' Mary says. 'He has looked down and noticed me, his humble servant, and my heart is bursting with laughter and with joy at this astounding thing which is happening.'

Second (and Christians do not like this sort of thing), she speaks about herself. She does not say 'we magnify the Lord' or 'we shall be called blessed.' She says '*me*'. Six times in that short first section of the Magnificat she refers to herself: 'My soul . . . my spirit . . . his handmaiden . . . me . . . generations shall call me blessed . . . he has magnified me.'

It sounds self-centred, and in a way it is. It is an honest and open acknowledgement of what God is doing with her: one chosen person caught up in the excitement and creativity of almighty God. That Magnificat prayer should stand for all time against the excessive self-denial that religion so often encourages in people.

How often are we led to believe that we must deny our own worth, our own giftedness and our own potential, under the mistaken assumption that this is what God wants? All too often we are left with that grey shadow of the person whom God, in the richness and colour of his love, creates us to be.

We may be called to avoid self-indulgence, but that can all too often become a humbler-than-thou self-indulgence itself. Maybe when the Christ person commanded us to love our neighbour 'as ourselves' he really meant us to love ourselves too. After all, if we do not love and value ourselves, will we really be able to love and value other people?

To love someone is to actively seek their well-being, even if that person is oneself.

Mary seems to be saying: 'I have just realized how much I am loved by God. I am given meaning and significance by that love and my heart is full of laughter and thanksgiving that this is happening. My heart rejoices: I am glad to be me.'

But the third reason why this Magnificat prayer is important is the one we are really after. It comes in the words: 'From henceforth all generations shall call me blessed.' Why should all generations call this peasant girl blessed from this moment onwards? Because from this moment something is going to be different. From this moment, salvation is no longer a mystery. The Pete Stoodley moment has arrived.

Before that young peasant woman drew breath to utter that beautiful Old Testament prayer of thanksgiving, the meaning and course of life was unclear. Her nation had been led into its Promised Land and, in the course of its history, this community of faith had come closer to the mind and heart of God than any other people on earth. Time and time again they had fallen into error and damaged their relationship of trust in God. And time and time again they had been forgiven and restored.

But then there had come a time when, for hundreds of years, it seemed that there was only a great silence. The voice of God was not heard. Their sacred land was invaded by the pagan Roman Empire and God's gift to them was desecrated. It was a time of anger, guilt, confusion and turmoil.

The will of God was indeed a mystery; and the will of God was life. Their hopes and expectations ranged from outbursts of bitter guerrilla warfare to fawning political compromise. And who was to say which was right?

Partly out of desperation and partly out of faith, there developed a growing hope that a deliverer would come. He would rescue them from the army of occupation and restore God's gift of the land to its rightful tenants. And, in truth, a deliverer did come. But few (if any) expected the intervention of God to happen in the way that it did.

Salvation was at hand. But not the salvation that most people expected and hoped for. Life was being given by God for the whole world in a great and generous act of love. Salvation was no longer a mystery. Salvation was at that moment developing in a young girl's womb.

The Christ-child was not born that we should have mystery, although a sense of mystery can be an important part of worship. He was born that we might have life. But it was the working out of that life (foreshadowed by the concluding words of the Magnificat) which was to prove the problem.

9 DECEMBER
Conflicting images

———————◆———————

One of the most effective ways of recovering from the trauma of Christmas shopping is to visit the London Planetarium.

This giant-size magic-lantern show sounds a bit boring at first. You sit in reclining seats in the dark and look up at pin-points of light that shine in the ceiling. Each point of light accurately represents a star in the sky. But as you lie back in your seat, it only takes a few moments to become utterly enthralled by the unfolding story of the universe.

What really hits you is the stark contrast between the vastness of the universe and the insignificant size of our own little planet.

You become lost in the sheer size of the universe. Our world is part of the solar system; the solar system is a tiny part of our galaxy of stars; and there are hundreds or thousands (or is it millions?) of galaxies in the universe.

Suddenly you realize that, in terms of size, distance and the silent passing of billions of years, we are nothing. It puts that Christmas shopping in context in a very powerful way.

But it also brings home how people in the ancient world might have viewed the stars. Technology has long since shrunk the world to nothing more than a global village, and it is difficult to get far enough away from the bright lights of civilization to actually see the stars in the night sky.

But how did that same night sky look to the ancient world? To the person who wrote Psalm 8, for example? Imagine them lying on their back on a hillside, gazing up at the heavens, and, in the darkness and the silence, thinking those immortal words: 'When I look up at thy heavens, the work of thy fingers, the moon and the stars set in their places by thee, what is man that thou shouldst remember him, mortal man that thou shouldst care for him?' (Psalm 8:3).

We need to remember that same sense of awe and wonder when we read the words of Mary's Magnificat prayer, because it brings together two powerful and conflicting images. It was the collision of these images which ultimately led the Christ person to the cross.

The first image is that of God in power and majesty: 'he that is mighty has magnified me,' says Mary, 'and holy is his name.' The Magnificat is a prayer of awe and wonder, a prayer of recognition that God is the one who has created the vastness of the heavens, the millions upon millions of stars – and the little world in which we live.

'Holy,' she says in awed reverence, 'is his name.' She too has looked up at the night sky, of which the London Planetarium is but a pale shadow, and she has glimpsed the grandeur of God and the utter vastness of creation.

But then, in the next line of the Magnificat, come these contrasting images:

> He has scattered the proud in the imagination of their
> hearts.
> He has put down the mighty from their seats
> and has exalted the humble and meek.
> He has filled the hungry with good things, and the
> rich he has sent away empty.
>
> (Luke 1:51–3, RSV)

Suddenly we have moved from the sublime to the ridiculous. One moment we are struck dumb by the vastness and the awesome majesty of God, and the next we are being told that this same awesome God has a particular and passionate concern for the poorest inhabitants of our tiny planet.

Is this seriously part of the story of the Christ-child? Or is it a bit of religious tradition that has accidentally become tangled up with the gospel story?

To be honest, there is no way of proving that Mary actually said the words of the Magnificat. But, whether or not she said them, they are totally in keeping with the sayings and events of the life of the Christ person. And these words bring into sharp focus a vital thread running through both the Old and New Testaments of the Bible. We need to hold on to the Magnificat, not just because it is the prayer of thanksgiving by the mother of the Christ-child, but, more importantly, because it is a core statement about the nature and purpose of God's love.

We can test this out, first by listening to the words of Christ himself and, second, by looking back over the Old Testament. And what happens when we do that?

We see that this Christ person gets himself into all sorts of trouble with the religious authorities by associating with the poor and the outcasts of his own day. They were regarded as sinful and unclean and it was forbidden for a religious person – especially a religious teacher – to have anything to do with them. To do so would be to become defiled and unclean, and therefore not in a fit state to worship God.

But the whole story of Jesus is littered with accounts of him going out of his way to meet, befriend, touch and heal the very people that he, as a religious teacher, should be avoiding.

Not only that, he claimed that this outrageous behaviour actually reflected the will of God and the nature of his love. In Christ, God lifts up the humble and meek and the poor are fed, sometimes with physical food, but always with the nourishment of being respected, honoured and loved.

Like all of us, those we call the poor in our own society have a whole range of needs which have to be met if they are to live. But, above all, they need to be loved. If they are not loved, then all the hand-outs and luncheon vouchers in the world will not take away their hunger and their pain.

And, ironically, if we who are materially wealthy do not share our love with them, we too shall deny ourselves the gift of life. But that is a hard lesson to be learning so near to Christmas, the season of plenty.

10 DECEMBER

A short, sharp shock

---•---

Today we meet up with a very angry man called Amos. He was one of an important group of people in the Old Testament: the prophets.

Admittedly, words like 'Old Testament' and 'prophet' and even the name Amos sound old-fashioned to our ears. But all of these people, and Amos in particular, were saying things that are amazingly relevant as we begin our new millennium 2,500 years later.

For a start, Amos didn't mince his words and he wasn't afraid of upsetting people by telling them what he thought was on God's mind. You don't get pearls without grit.

And his book is certainly gritty. A mere 12 pages long, you can read it in as many minutes. But what it lacks in bulk it makes up for in clout. Written in about 750 BC, it must have been the original short, sharp shock.

The fact is that Amos wasn't much of a diplomat. A sheep farmer from a hilly area which bordered onto a desert, he was accustomed to a hard and dangerous life. Eking out a primitive existence 3,000 feet above sea-level, Amos looked down on civilization with growing anger.

Suddenly he abandons his sheep and comes down to the city to speak 'the Word' of the Lord God. And the Word is not a polite one: 'The Lord roars from Zion and thunders from Jerusalem. . . . The lion has roared; who is not terrified?' (Amos 1:2; 3:8).

Then, in a series of blistering attacks, each one mounting in intensity, he pours scorn on the six nations surrounding Israel for their vicious and inhuman ways. One nation, for example, has captured a king in battle. But instead of treating him with dignity as a prisoner of war, they have killed him, burned his body, crushed his bones to make lime, and then used the lime to plaster their walls.

The condemnation of such foreign atrocities would have delighted Amos' fellow countrymen. But, using a strategy that Jesus was to follow years later, Amos is setting a trap for them.

Far from pleasing his listeners, he is lulling them into a false sense of security, storing up his greatest condemnation for his own people. But it is an anger born out of anguish.

Time and time again, God has tried to love his people, but they have repeatedly rejected that love. 'Listen,' says Amos, 'to the words of the God who brought you out of slavery in Egypt, creating and nurturing you': 'For you alone have I cared among all the nations of the world; therefore I will punish you for your iniquities . . .' (3:2).

Five times God has warned his people, in a process that is mirrored by the story Jesus told about the wicked tenants. But, as in the Jesus story, the attempts at reconciliation come to nothing and the outcome is the same: the anger of God.

Sure enough, not long after the warning of Jesus, the Jewish nation was destroyed and the centre of its worship, the great Temple in Jerusalem, was reduced to rubble. So, too, after the warning by Amos, the nation was invaded by Assyria. These were not idle threats.

But why were these warnings from Amos necessary? Because, while the other nations were guilty of crimes against their enemies, God's own people were condemned for acts of inhumanity against each other, against their own people. And for rebellion against God.

In a time of great material prosperity, not unlike our own, what was going on? There was political and economic corruption. Many people lived in sumptuous wealth, while others lived in grinding poverty. And the whole system was supported by an underclass of slaves and peasants who had been thrown off the land. Land which had been a sacred gift from God for all his people.

The ancient practice of jubilee, according to which debts were cancelled at regular intervals, had gone out of the window. The divide between rich and poor seemed to be get-ting wider: 'They grind the heads of the poor into the earth and thrust the humble out of the way' (2:7). Therefore the luxurious 'houses of ivory shall perish and the great houses shall be demolished' (3:15).

Instead of celebrating the love of God and living in peace with their neighbour, the rich hold the poor in bondage. Trivial debts are used as an excuse to condemn the poor to a lifetime of servitude. Things have not changed: people in some parts of the world today are sold into industrial slavery and whole economies, and the price of our Christmas gifts, depend on child labour.

People live on the edge of starvation in places like India and Haiti, where workers are paid as little as 8 pence an hour to make fashion goods such as tee-shirts for our own children.

And what is to be God's response? As Mary said in her Magnificat prayer: the mighty shall be put down and the rich sent away empty. Like the threats of the angry Amos, the words of the Magnificat are not just to do with the ordering of society. They are also to do with the nature of our relationship with God. Industrial exploitation is a sin against the person of God, whose children we all are. It touches the heart of our spirituality.

This is hammered home in a particularly vitriolic passage where Amos describes God as being utterly nauseated by the worship that is offered to him: 'I hate and spurn your pil-grim feasts; I will not delight in your ceremonies. Spare me the sound of your songs,' roars God in anger (5:21-2).

So what sort of worship does God want of us? According to Amos it is: 'to let justice roll on like a river and righteous-ness like an ever-flowing stream' (5:24).

Love God and love your neighbour: the commands Jesus was to give centuries later.

All this may sound well and good. But, while anyone who has any compassion in their heart may agree with Amos and with his brother, the Christ person, a big question remains. If this is the will of God and if God is all-powerful, why are the poor still poor and the rich still feeding their faces? When is this big change going to come about – and how?

And the embarrassing answer is that there isn't an answer. One of the few useful things I remember about my theological training was how to reconcile two contradictory statements. You say: 'We need to hold these things in tension.' If that is so, there is a lot of tension around when it comes to social injustice.

All we can say is that Christians believe that from the time of Amos, from the moment of the Magnificat, from the moment Jesus hugged the leper and the father embraced the prodigal son, the will of God has been declared. It is like a signal for us. And maybe a challenge.

There was once a strip cartoon in which one frog says to the other: 'I want to ask God why he hasn't saved the poor and starving.' And the other frog says: 'Maybe that's what God wants to ask us.'

And maybe that is tomorrow's challenge.

11 DECEMBER
Not-so-happy families

If there's one word that is fashionable in the Church today it is the word 'family'. Whether it is family services in church, family values in society, two-parent families or the Holy Family, 'family' is the in word (as in 'happy families', of course).

But sometimes we seem a bit limited in our concept of the family: we tend to think of families like our own, as they are – or as they might have been. But the warm glow seems to cool just a little when we consider families of a different skin colour or ethnic origin – or of a different social class.

Yesterday we were exploring our relationship with God in the company of a very angry old man called Amos. Today we continue that process in the company of some angry young men – and women.

Just down the road from where I live in Leeds, the unemployment rate among young people is about 60 per cent. Many of these young people do not have a job, and most have no realistic chance of ever getting one.

Meanwhile, the area in which we live straddles a major commuter route into the city. Morning and night, wealthy people drive up and down that road in their new cars going to and from work. The young people often stand on the street corners and watch them go past.

What are the real options for these young people? To many of them the choice seems to be either to spend the next 40 years sitting in a benefits office each week, waiting to be paid a minimal and degrading hand-out, on which they certainly cannot live. Or to sell drugs and earn lots of money.

Of course, being a well-behaved citizen, I would take the

benefits hand-out, accept the degradation and injustice and keep quiet. I could do that with no trouble at all – for about three weeks. Then I would either explode or die of despair. Which is pretty well what the kids down the road do.

The rest of us know that this is going on, and that knowledge is painful. So what do we do? We try to avoid the pain. We do this by distancing ourselves from young people who are unemployed by blanket statements such as: 'The kids in that area are all criminals', 'Young people these days don't want to work', and 'Those sorts of people are just idle.'

The same sort of thing is also happening a couple of miles further down the road, but this time it's homeless people. Last year 400 young people were classified by our city council as being homeless and in need of urgent help. Another 1,200 were registered as being homeless at some stage during the same 12 months. A church-sponsored survey of the city found that on an average night 140 homeless families were chasing just seven available and appropriate privately rented flats or houses.

Now this is serious guilt-trip material. How are we going to side-step this one?

First, with the help of the tabloid press, who are only too happy to describe homeless people as scum and parasites and, above all, to claim that homeless people have only themselves to blame for their plight. Add the inevitable story of the beggar with a new Rolls Royce round the corner, and we are feeling better already.

But, in our hearts, we know these tabloid caricatures of homeless and unemployed people are untrue. So, undaunted, we try a different avoidance strategy. 'Yes, of course it's terrible. Yes, of course we would like to help,' we tell ourselves. 'No, of course no one wants to see people living on the streets. But there just isn't the money. We only wish there was.'

The trouble with that excuse is that, like the tabloid argument, it isn't true. Look at some of the basic facts.

The single most important cause of homelessness is the lack of affordable social housing. Over a period of 15 years central government spending on housing has dropped from £13 billion to £5 billion. But even £5 billion is a huge amount of money, we may argue. Five thousand million pounds.

But last year in the weeks before Christmas we as a nation spent £7 billion on presents, food and drink – over and above our normal weekly shopping bills. Basically, we care more about Christmas crackers than we do about homeless people.

In Leeds alone in the last five years, £1 billion has been invested in the city centre. More than £70 million is currently being spent by High Street retailers on their premises; £3 million has been spent on one super-pub and another £5 million spent on a new night-club that holds more than 3,000 people.

Sitting in the rain, the homeless person sees all this. They may be wet and cold, but they are not stupid. The bright lights of the offices and shops, the pubs and the clubs, simply make the cold and the rain harder to bear.

At the moment there are about 350,000 homeless people in Britain, and the number of young people who are becoming homeless, often as a result of benefits changes, has recently been pushing this figure steadily higher.

But who are these people? Not the romantic, weather-beaten gentlemen of the road of yester-year. These are people who were in care as children and seldom had the blessing of love and personal attention. They are often people with a mental illness or disability who are now experiencing the reality of care in the community. They are people who have been sexually or physically abused as children, either within the family or in local authority care. They are former members of the armed forces who have served Queen and country, but then found themselves with no home and no experience of fending for themselves. And no job.

More than half of the people sleeping rough in Britain are suffering from at least one serious physical illness, an increasing number from tuberculosis. More than a third have a severe mental illness which may make them a danger to themselves, and sometimes to other people. They are people who suffer from clinical depression and are often too frightened or insecure to stay in the hostels that are provided, in case they are attacked or abused by other clients.

Among this group, the largest single cause of death is suicide and the average age of death is 42 years.

Who are these people? They are people living in Hell. And they are our sisters and brothers in Christ. And if God is our Father, then they are members of our own Holy Family. They are people who feel pain and despair. They are people who have intelligence, wisdom, courage and humour. Above all, they are the Magnificat people.

Today the words of that Magnificat are lost on the wind and swept aside by the tides of shoppers who worship another god: Mammon. Year by year we complain that Christmas seems to start sooner and sooner.

We seldom realize how early Good Friday comes for some people.

A cry for help

————•————

It may sound surprising, but associating with people who have no secure home life brings many profound blessings as you are accepted into a generous and loving fellowship. For once, you are not judged.

A priest who was asked by one of his superiors what it was exactly that he did with homeless people replied that he spent his time loafing around enjoying the company of his betters.

Tragically, however, such friendships can be brief. All too often you find yourself at the funeral of another friend who has died.

You might be forgiven for assuming that the funeral of someone who had very little by way of material wealth would be a very threadbare affair. In truth, they sometimes are like that, but often the opposite is true.

Two of the homeless men I knew who have died in the recent past were both called John – Big John and Little John. And their funerals were as memorable as the men themselves, but for rather different reasons.

Little John's funeral took place in one of the most beautiful churches in the city. Robin, the parish priest, had known Little John well, and he had a good idea who would be at the service.

At the front of the church he had set out a glass-topped table with some unlit night-light candles on it. John's coffin was carried in and the service began. But, instead of giving a formal address, Robin invited people to come up to the front of the church and say a few words about what Little

John had meant to them. Then they were invited to light one of the small candles on the table.

First a couple of clergy came up and said a few words. Then they each lit a candle and sat down. Next, one or two other people came forward. But then the whole service seemed to blossom as more and more people, many of whom had probably never spoken in public before, stood to honour their friend in words which rang with love and sincerity.

Suddenly the few little candles on the table had become a sea of light and praise. The tears rolled down creased and weathered faces as we remembered Little John with his corny jokes, his quiet voice and his gentle courtesy to everyone.

No pope or archbishop ever had a send-off like that. It was a day to remember, just as gentle Little John was a man to remember.

For a long time after that there were no funerals, and for a time it seemed we were beginning to prove the statistics wrong. But then, without warning, Big John died.

He had had a terrible life. His parents had died when he was very young. When I heard that, I thought back to another little boy of about the same age. I wondered who had broken the news to John that day and whether it had been a sunny April morning, too.

Whatever pain John's life had brought him, it was over now. His funeral was memorable for a number of reasons, not least for the words of Big John himself. This is what he had written just a few years earlier. It was read out at the funeral by a friend.

John's testimony

Today I can only give thanks to God and the Lord Jesus my saviour for rescuing me and bringing me into life.

I was born in Liverpool forty-six years ago. My father died at an early age of cirrhosis of the liver from alcohol abuse, and my mother followed shortly after of a broken heart. I was left to be brought up by foster parents and was sent to a Catholic school in Ireland. I left school at fifteen and a half years old and went back to Liverpool.

I worked for four years with the Army in Wiltshire and married at the age of twenty-one and had two lovely daughters.

Drugs and alcohol took their toll on my life from then onward and I got into many terrible situations in life. This came to a head when men came to collect money I owed them for my drug-taking habit. These men came at me in a dance hall and as I tried to avoid them they stabbed my wife. She died a few days later and from that time onward I went into a real decline.

I attacked one of these attackers and was prosecuted and put into jail for a sentence of five years. They remitted my sentence and I served three and a half years.

My sin life didn't stop there but escalated and went from bad to worse. Drinking and every form of drug abuse pursued me constantly. But I knew there was something more from life.

In 1979 I came to Leeds to stay. I had been moving up and down the country wandering from place to place. No fixed abode. Desolate and very unhappy outside St George's Crypt in 1990 I cried out to God: 'O God, there must be something more. Lord, if you are there, do something for me.'

Some weeks later I was drunk and falling about in the Merrion Centre when I saw a man I later got to know as Malcolm. He spoke to me about Jesus but I didn't understand. Then a lady called Dawn came up and spoke the things of God to me and then I did begin to understand. God was answering my cry for help. These people were telling me that God cared for me.

Several days later I gave my life to the Lord Jesus Christ and my life has totally changed ever since. Today I serve the Lord Jesus Christ with all my life and I have got a flat in Leeds. I am looking for work and write and draw for Jesus.

He has changed me from a nothing into a something.
He has delivered me from death and given me eternal
    life.
I am so grateful to Him for everything and grateful
    that His servants are obedient to hear his voice and
    go into the streets and help people like me.
Now I am helping to do the same thing for others.

Staggering around outside a city drop-in centre, a homeless
man cries out to God. And around him in one of the richest
cities in the country people are spending millions in the
night-clubs, pubs, restaurants and shops.

Desolate and very unhappy, Big John prayed with all his
heart. In a way, he had nothing to lose. He had long since
lost everything. And it was into that emptiness that God
gently poured his love. Sometimes when we are so low that
we are scraping the bottom of the barrel we come up against
the wood of the Cross.

Emptiness and love: two of the things at the centre of
what our own journey is all about. The question is, dare we
risk the emptiness in order to receive the love?

The duckling detector

————◆————

Despite a very unsettled childhood, or maybe because of it, some memories stand out clear and sweet. One of them is listening to the wireless on Saturday mornings and hearing Danny Kaye tell the story of the ugly duckling. Do you remember it?

One day there was trouble in the farmyard. One of the ducklings was a different colour from the others and his brothers and sisters didn't like the look of him. So the ugly duckling was thrown out. Like others who are homeless, he found a place to hide and tried to keep warm during the long winter. Then one day a flight of swans passed overhead. One of them glanced down at the ugly duckling and shouted: 'Hey, you're a good looking swan!'

'I'm not a swan, I'm an ugly duckling' our hero shouted back. 'Oh, yes?' said the magnificent swan circling above him. 'That's not how I see it. Take a look at yourself some time.'

To most people in Britain today, Big John and Little John were ugly ducklings. Jesus was certainly an ugly duckling. And, in a way, our whole faith story, from long before angry old Amos, is the real-life story of the ugly duckling.

Time and time again we see different people being kicked out of the farmyard by the other ducklings because their feathers are different. But, time and time again in the Gospels, we hear the word that these little people are not the scum of the earth: they are swans. That's how God sees it.

Or is that just wishful thinking?

Whether or not our faith story is just a fairy story we shall never know, this side of the grave. That's why faith is such a

46

high-risk venture. But what we do know is that the theory of the ugly duckling, in terms of God's special concern for the poor and the vulnerable, has been around for a very long time.

Lost on the streets of a northern city, Big John cried out: 'O God, there must be something more. Lord, if you are there, do something for me.'

There seemed to be only silence. But, in that cry, John was echoing thousands of years of other cries of anguish and pain. And in the months and years ahead he was to sense an answer to that prayer. Or did he imagine it all? It is possible that he did imagine it. But if he did, then he was following a long and noble tradition.

If we root around among the source documents of faith and delve into the story of the community in which the Christ person lived, we suddenly notice something quite remarkable. Again and again we see the ugly duckling story happening in real life.

Let's take three examples.

The first is a story we have already touched on: the account of how that original community came into existence. According to the most treasured tradition, the nation was created by God by being delivered out of slavery in Egypt and led into what was believed to be the Promised Land.

The people who were treated like ugly ducklings by their foreign masters were brought into new life and told that they were nothing less than a chosen people, called to share in the work of God himself. The Exodus is a creation story: from ugly duckling to swan.

The second example concerns the greatest king the nation ever had: David. As we have discovered, David had a very poor personal track record. Seduction, adultery and murder feature prominently on his CV. And if his personal life was less than perfect, his political life also had its problems. In common with any political person, he had enemies who were out to get him.

But one of the most important things David seems to have done was to write many of the Psalms. These were, and are, the hymns of the community. While the origins of most of

them are lost in the mists of time, many are attributed to
David. Above all, the Psalms are a treasure-house of the
community's experience of God. So where does the ugly
duckling come into all this?

Look what happens when we run the duckling detector
over the Psalms: of the first 72, called the Psalms of David,
no fewer than 52 contain ugly-duckling references. That is,
these Psalms either express God's care for the poor and outcast, or describe David himself in an ugly-duckling situation
of danger, exclusion and vulnerability. In the remaining 78
Psalms, there are 35 ugly-duckling references.

We could argue, therefore, that the ugly-duckling factor
runs right through this collection of stories, songs and
prayers which are at the heart of the community's experience
of God. But care for the poor is not just a matter of compassion for the weak; it is a matter of justice and of the very
nature of God's relationship with us.

Take an example from Psalm 72 (verses 1, 4 and 14):

> O God, endow the king with thy own justice . . .
> That he might judge the people rightly
> and deal out justice to the poor and suffering.
> He shall give judgement for the suffering
> and help those of the people who are needy;
> he shall crush the oppressor.
> May he redeem them from oppression and violence
> and may their blood be precious in his eyes.

Third and finally, we encounter one of the greatest figures of
the Old Testament. This is the person we know as Isaiah.

The collection of writings that make up the 'Book' of Isaiah
were almost certainly written at different times by as many
as three different people. Bad news for the historians, but all
the better for us. It gives us a wider sweep of history and
reduces the chances of our sample being unrepresentative.

There are 66 chapters in Isaiah and in 26 of them there
are significant ugly-duckling references to the poor and justice for the poor. Not as many references as in the Psalms,

you may say? But what astounding references they are. Here are just a few:

> You [the elders of the people] have ravished the vineyard,
> and the spoils of the poor are in your houses.
> Is it nothing that you crush my people
> and grind the faces of the poor?
>
> (Isaiah 3:14)

> Shame on you who make unjust laws . . .
> depriving the poor of justice,
> robbing the weakest of my people of their rights,
> despoiling the widow and plundering the orphan.
>
> (Isaiah 10:2)

> Is this not what I require of you . . . to unloose
> the fetters of injustice, to snap every yoke
> and set free those who have been crushed?

> Is it not sharing your food with the hungry,
> taking the homeless poor into your house,
> clothing the naked when you meet them?
>
> (Isaiah 58:6)

It's powerful stuff. But there is yet more. If we just step back from this for a moment, we suddenly see something else going on in Isaiah. In this great collection of writings a strange figure seems to emerge. He appears in five separate sections of Isaiah in what are called the Servant Songs. This servant figure is not named and remains indistinct. But he has a powerful message, and it is one that will be taken up years later by the servant figure of the Christ person.

Staggering down a street in a northern industrial city, a man cries out: 'O God, there must be something more. Lord, if you are there, do something for me.'

And thundering down the centuries comes the voice of the servant figure from Isaiah:

> The Spirit of the Lord God is upon me:
> he has sent me to bring good news to the humble,

> to bind up the broken-hearted,
> to proclaim liberty to the captives
> and release to those in prison;
> to proclaim the year of the Lord's favour.
>
> (Isaiah 61:1)

No wonder Big John would later write his own creation psalm, summing up the wisdom of the Old Testament and the good news of the New Testament in a single sentence:

> He has changed me from a nothing into a something.
> He has delivered me from death and given me eternal life.

At a distance a swan looks a rather docile bird. But a closer encounter reveals it to be a creature of immense power. The same may be true of God.

14 DECEMBER

Imperfect harmony

———◆———

It was the middle of December and the Sunday morning service was late starting. There was a problem: the organist was ill and had not turned up. Finally it was agreed that Winifred would play instead.

Winifred was in her seventies and a capable pianist. But playing an organ is different, as it soon became clear. The first hymn was a disaster. The vicar had a choice, and he made the wrong one. Instead of abandoning the organ and asking her to play the piano which stood nearby, he ploughed on in the hope that things would get better. Things did not get better.

Two rows from the back, a friend of mine was singing through gritted teeth. But then something rather odd happened. Later he told me:

The first hymn was hell. If there were any newcomers in church that day, they must have thought we were mad.

When we started into the second hymn I was ready for walking out. She managed to hit about one right note in four. But, if I'm honest, I suppose she was getting most of them right. Anyway, it wasn't her fault; she wasn't an organist. Just doing her best.

Then I suddenly thought about how many things I get wrong in life. I stood there thinking about how my life would sound if it were set to music; or if God was keeping a score of my wrong notes, the way I was counting Winifred's.

After a couple more verses her playing didn't seem so bad. Maybe I was thinking more about the notes she got

51

right than the other ones. After the service I told her: 'You taught me something there today, Winifred.'

Funny, I can't remember what the sermon was about that day.

A lot of people who are homeless today carry not only the physical burden of not having a secure place to live; they often carry a huge burden of guilt. It may be a sense of remorse for something that has happened in the past: a broken marriage or someone they have let down.

I am sure that one reason why I feel so comfortable and cared for by the homeless people I am privileged to know arises out of my own sense of failure in life. But with these people, I find that I am not being judged. There is a bond of friendship and acceptance which for some of us, I suspect, arises naturally out of a mutual sense of failure.

Some people are addicted to work and some people are addicted to drink, and often both are to do with the need to take away the emotional and spiritual pain.

Sometimes the shallow waters of a casual conversation will suddenly deepen into a question about punishment and what God is really like. And who am I to say? All I can try to do is to try to be honest about my own experience and point to the one who seems to know better than most of us the answer to that question.

A small incident has helped me to make sense of this business of guilt and what the Church calls sin. It happened at a Communion service. I must have heard the words of the confession and absolution a thousand times, but there are two words which had never quite registered. The assurance of forgiveness speaks not simply of us being pardoned of our sins, but pardoned and delivered from them.

That 'delivered' bit had never quite sunk in with me. 'Pardoned' sounds like a fixed-point event, but 'delivered' has the idea of movement attached to it. The Christmas cards which have started to arrive each day are delivered by the postman. They move from one place to another. Suddenly I began to grasp what might be going on.

We are pardoned from our mistakes and our sins by the unconditional love of God, and that is something profoundly amazing and wonderful. But God may not have quite finished with us.

God is the God of dynamic creation, constantly leading us forward into new life. The Church is not greatly attracted to change, but God is different. God seems to be saying not just that we are forgiven, but that we are given a new opportunity to live.

There is a dynamic forward movement going on here: we are given the courage to acknowledge our failings and we are gifted with love and forgiveness by God. But then he says: 'Get on with the rest of your life. Don't stay sitting there in that shell-hole among the rubble of the past – move on.' Somewhere St Paul says something about leaving behind what is past and pressing forward to that which lies ahead.

This doesn't mean pretending the past has not happened; it means acknowledging our mistakes – and then getting on with our lives. Does the God who loves us really want us to be forever imprisoned in our guilt?

Even the man in the congregation didn't keep a count of Winifred's wrong notes, at least after the first hymn. He was able to think about just how many she was getting right. He had moved on. And after the service he gave her a big hug and told her how courageous she had been. And they both moved on.

But how do we know this? How did Paul know this? Where does this idea come from? Maybe it comes from the Christ-child, whose birth now draws close to us. Our journey is moving on; the Christ-child will be born and will move on.

The love of God so majestically declared in John's gospel is not static, but moves forward: 'God so loved the world'. How does he love it? Is that a static statement of good will and affection? No, he loves it 'so much that he gave us his only son' so that we might move forward into life.

Then it begins to dawn on us that in the gospel accounts of the life of the Christ person, the same pattern of forward movement is being played out. Let's take three examples.

Jesus heals the lepers, and immediately sends them to the priest for the rite of cleansing. They move on, from the point of cleansing, forward into their own lives.

The paralysed man is healed. Lying on the stretcher which his crazy friends have lowered through a hole in the roof where Jesus is teaching, he is forgiven his sins and healed of his paralysis. Wonderful. But Jesus has not quite finished with him. 'Take up your bed and go back to your own life,' he says. 'Leave behind this event and this past existence. Forget the hole in the roof; we'll sort that out later.'

Finally, let's take the most important example of this process of moving forward: the Crucifixion itself. Jesus is nailed to the Cross. There is no fixed point more static than that, except perhaps the tomb in which he is to be laid and sealed with a boulder. But even now God is not static. Suddenly the frightened group of disciples are charged with a new vision and power, and something is different. The Resurrection is the classic example of moving on: from death into life.

God is always tugging at us, urging us to have the courage to move on. Maybe that is why we are making this strange Advent journey of ours – and why Luke wrote his gospel, as we will discover tomorrow.

15 DECEMBER
The big risk

———◆———

One of the most memorable events of childhood is learning to ride a bicycle. I can vividly remember the day it happened to me. Riding a bicycle is simple. But, like many of the simple things in life, it is not easy.

I remember sitting astride what seemed a very large and unstable bicycle, while my father walked beside me holding onto the back of the saddle so that I did not fall off. One day I said, as I often did: 'Don't let go, Dad.' But this time there was no reassuring answer. He wasn't there. He was some distance back along the road. I immediately panicked and fell off. But I had cracked it and soon I was tearing around on two wheels with the others, wondering why I had ever bothered with a kid's three-wheeler.

There is something about personal experience and discovery which changes our outlook on life. What we hear, we tend to forget. What we see, we sometimes remember. But it is the things we do that become part of our lives.

Luke's gospel begins with a very odd statement. He says: 'Many other people have written this Christ story down, so I have decided to as well.' But, if other people had already done the job, why did he want to do it all over again? It would have made more sense to say: 'A lot of other people have done this, so there is no need for me to bother.' What was the point of repeating the exercise?

Perhaps there were three reasons for Luke to write what has been called the most beautiful book in the world. The first reason is clear from the opening words of the gospel. He says: 'I want to give the most careful and accurate account of what happened. This story is so important that it is vital to make sure we get it right.' But what might this 'getting it right' mean? Has someone been getting it wrong?

The second possible reason for Luke to write his gospel is what the bookmakers might call a very long shot. But look at it this way: Luke starts writing his gospel round about the year AD 57 in a town called Caesarea. For the past ten years he has been a companion of St Paul, who was one of the leading figures in the early church. Paul is best known for spreading the Christian faith outside Israel in the Gentile world, and for writing the 'letters' which make up about half the New Testament.

But where is Paul when Luke suddenly emerges from obscurity and starts writing? Paul is in jail, and effectively silenced. So what is happening?

When I read Paul I hear a man talking to established Christian groups. Although he is opening up the Christian faith to the entire Gentile world, these little churches are quite definite and exclusive groups. He speaks about the community of faith and about the Church being the 'body' of Christ. He discourages people inside those communities from marrying people outside. The language is significantly 'us and them'. He talks about life on the 'human level' and life on the 'spiritual' level: about creation groaning in travail and 'the shackles of mortality'. Meanwhile he looks forward to the spiritual 'splendour that is in store for us'.

Who are the 'us'? People inside the stockade of faith? And what about those on the outside? They are people liable to encounter the wrath and retribution of God, he says, even those who have never even heard of Jesus and the Gospel. The powerful images are often of judgement and punishment.

But when I read Luke, the music is different. His images are inclusive. Sinners and outcasts are embraced warmly and unconditionally by the Christ person. We receive crucial insights into the nature of God's love through prostitutes and prodigal sons; through despised Samaritans and the sinner in the Temple. Luke, in contrast to Paul, describes the fellowship of Christ as an open and accessible friendship, not a religious group with controlled boundaries.

Paul seems to hate the flesh, but in Luke, the Christ person seems to quite like the flesh. He is always touching other people's, in healing, or sharing food in friendship and love. Paul rages against drunkards and gluttons, but Jesus, in cynical humour, describes himself as being one. Paul aches for the world to come: the Christ of the gospels is busy living in this one.

As we turn the pages of the New Testament, Luke comes before Paul. But that can be misleading: Luke was writing after Paul, and with a certain knowledge of what Paul had said. It is only after Paul has been imprisoned that Luke emerges from obscurity to write his gospel. Do we hear in this an echo of Jesus emerging from obscurity after John the Baptist has been imprisoned?

Luke was writing after Paul. Is it possible that what he wrote was a counterbalance to some of the things Paul seemed to emphasize? Both were writing for the Gentile world. Did Luke think that Paul's imaging of the Christ person was less than complete? Was that one reason he took up his pen?

The third reason for Luke to write his gospel brings us down to earth, and back to bicycles. Who is Luke writing for? Obviously, for the person he calls Theophilus, to whom the gospel is addressed. But it is also written, I suspect, for Luke himself. As with many books, it is the author's own journey of discovery.

Of course Luke could have passively accepted what others had written about the Christian faith. And sometimes the Church seems to want us, in our own age, to do just that. The Church seems to say: 'We've worked it all out. You just sit there and believe it. Better minds than yours have sorted out all this complicated doctrine and theology. You just take the God-tablets and everything will be fine.'

But everything will not be fine. It will be three-wheeler religion: quiet, respectable, safe and peaceful. It will be sterile and dead.

The trouble is that the Jesus we encounter in Luke's gospel is none of those things. Instead, Luke reveals to us a Christ person born in danger and chaos, and bursting with vitality and controversy. A person offering us not three-wheeler religion but two-wheeler life.

Naturally, most parents worry about their children. On a tricycle in the garden you are safe. Mummy can see you. But, on a two-wheeler, things are different. Suddenly the garden isn't big enough and, without warning, you are out of the gate and down the road. Out of Mummy's sight and control.

Maybe that's one of the big hang-ups the Church has. It wants to be Mummy and it wants things to be safe. It wants the Gospel to be safe and it wants Christmas to be safe. But, if we are honest, neither of them is safe.

The Advent adventure is a dangerous one. It exposes us to risk: the risk of hearing things we don't want to hear, being led into discoveries that will endanger our life-style and our bank balance.

As long as the Christ-child stays on the Christmas card and we stay in the garden on our tricycle, everything is safe. But that's not good enough for Luke. He wants to discover for himself what this Christ person is all about. And if we want to do the same, like him, we shall be taking a great journey into the unknown.

16 DECEMBER

A life-and-death decision

———◆———

The bicycle idea raises some disturbing questions for us on our Advent adventure. For a start, we never really thought this was an adventure, just a matter of reading another religious book. But the gospel is not just a story from the past, it is an event which challenges us here and now. The question is: are we going to take the bicycle risk of faith, or are we content to remain a spectator?

At first the journey of faith seems easy. We have some good companions on the way, like Luke and his fellow writer, Matthew. Like my Dad holding onto the saddle of my bike to stop me falling over, they too are walking beside us.

But there comes a time when we need more space. We need them to let go and allow us the freedom to get onto the open road, and run the risk of falling off, at least a couple of times.

That suddenly sounds quite a lonely proposition. Maybe we need to look around, not for someone to hold our hand or steady the bicycle, but at least to speak a word of reassurance. Someone to say: 'It's OK. I've tried it, and it works.'

Let's see what happens when we encounter such a person in a story which Luke himself tells us.

Once upon a time there was a Roman soldier. We do not know his name, but he was a centurion, a man in charge of 100 soldiers, in the imperial army. One day there is an emergency.

A servant for whom the centurion cares deeply is desperately ill and close to death. The doctors can do nothing.

Suddenly the centurion, who is a wealthy man and an officer in the Roman army of occupation, is powerless.

Faced with the approaching death of someone he loves and values, the centurion is driven to a desperate course of action. Calling some of his Jewish friends, he asks them to go with all haste to the Christ person. Perhaps he will be able to save the servant where the medical experts have failed.

The centurion's friends hurry off to find Jesus. Time is of the essence. But after they have gone, what happens? Perhaps the centurion sits at the servant's bedside, willing him to live at least until Jesus arrives. The minutes tick by.

We think back to a young father at the hospital bedside of his dying wife. The doctors could do nothing. How did he feel in those last fateful hours and minutes? What message would he have sent to the Christ person?

As the minutes tick by and the centurion waits, something dawns on the Roman soldier. He rushes to the door and issues another order. A second servant is dispatched to find Jesus. The first message said: 'Come quickly.' The second message says: 'Don't come.'

Don't come? What has happened? Has the servant died? Is it all too late? No, the servant is still lying close to death on the bed. The last minutes of his life are ticking steadily away.

What has happened? The centurion has not given up. He has made a discovery about the Christ person. The first message said: 'You are a healer. You may be able to help. Come quickly.'

The second message says: 'Do not trouble to come. Do not lower yourself to come into my Gentile house. I am not worthy to have you under my roof. Just speak the word and my servant will be healed.'

Is this really happening? This is an officer of the imperial Roman army sending word to a untidy, vagrant Jewish preacher.

'Just give the word of command,' says the centurion, 'and I know that my servant will live. Why? Because I am a person in authority and under authority. I say to one soldier: "Come," and he comes. I say to another one: "Go," and he goes.'

Suddenly, sitting in the quietness at the bedside of his dying servant, the centurion has realized who Jesus is. The centurion is under the authority of the emperor in Rome, the supreme ruler of the whole civilized world. And it is from the emperor that he derived his own authority as a centurion. In a sudden flash of realization, he makes the astounding connection about authority and the Christ person.

It dawns on him that Jesus is also under authority, but an authority which is greater even than that of the emperor. 'Only speak the word,' he says, 'and that word will be obeyed, just as in a different way my command would also be obeyed. Just say the word, nothing more, and my servant will live.'

What an astounding gamble. What awesome confidence that man had. Waiting at the deathbed of someone he loves, the realization bursts upon him that Jesus is a person in supreme authority.

But how do we know this was such a staggering leap of faith? Because Jesus himself tells us. Luke says that when the Christ person received the centurion's second message he was astounded. And in his amazement he says of this pagan soldier: 'Never among the whole people of God have I ever seen such faith.' It is the highest praise that we ever hear on his lips, and it is spoken of a foreigner whose troops have occupied and desecrated the Promised Land.

And Luke tells us that at that moment the servant is healed.

What was happening there? The centurion could have read books about Jesus until the end of time without discovering who he was. It was only in the real-life situation that he realized the significance of this vagrant healer. Though he had never met him, the centurion suddenly knew who the Christ person was.

In only one other place in the gospels do we encounter a centurion, and he is standing at the foot of a cross. This time

it is not a dying servant or a dying mother, but a dying son.
All through the execution, the centurion stands at his post.
He is a professional soldier. He is under authority. But then
he breaks ranks.

As one of the criminals dies, he suddenly bursts out with
words of disobedience and insurrection: 'Surely, this man
was the Son of God.'

Or was it: 'This man was a son of God'? Or perhaps he
said: 'This man was innocent.' All three appear as variations
on the text. And, anyway, who was taking notes? His words
were carried away on the wind and we shall never know.

Was it the same centurion? Probably not. But probably
you cannot balance a bicycle on two wheels.

It is only in trusting that we learn to trust. Only by risking
falling off the bicycle that we learn to ride and discover the
freedom of the open road. Only by being willing to enter
into the Advent adventure of this Christ story will we be
gifted with life. And that is more than probable.

17 DECEMBER

The Darnall Dog

◆

A recent opinion poll put journalists, along with politicians, at the bottom of the league table of trustworthiness. But it was not always so, and journalists, especially local and regional journalists, are usually very responsible people. Even when it means allowing the facts to ruin a good story.

Take, for example, the Saga of the Darnall Dog.

A reporter and photographer were once sent out to cover a dog story in the Darnall area of Sheffield. The story was that a much-loved pet dog had been condemned to Death Row by heartless neighbours. Their task was to interview the heartbroken owner of the condemned dog. On the way the photographer kept muttering about soft-focus shots.

They arrived at the house, which was on a busy road, and knocked on the door. A noise came from inside the house which sounded like the Hound of Hell breaking loose. The door was opened and a yellow-eyed slavering brute of a dog tore past the terrified journalists and into the road – and attacked an oncoming car.

They watched in amazement as it chased the car down the road, snarling and yelping as it tried to bite its tyres. The reporter and photographer beat a hasty retreat before the Devil Dog from Darnall could turn its attention to them. There were no soft-focus shots. The news editor was furious, but they had to be honest: there was no story.

There is a fine, if somewhat dented, tradition among journalists that the facts are sacred. And it may be that the facts were sacred to many of the early Christians. When there was a good chance that you might be arrested and put to death for your beliefs, you probably thought quite carefully about just what it was you believed in. And why make up a story if it is likely to cost you your life?

Similarly with the people who wrote the gospels: it's hard enough trying to write a book with the help of a word processor, central heating and endless cups of tea. But why bother writing a gospel, when it took so much time and effort to write anything in those days?

People like Luke and Matthew almost certainly didn't get everything right, but they probably did their best to tell the story of the Christ person in a way that was truthful. They wanted to encourage other people to explore the truth and that no doubt influenced the way they wrote. But there would not be much point in risking their lives to get other people to believe something that was unreal.

But Luke and Matthew weren't the first reporters on the scene. St Mark beat them by a good few years. So what happened? In true journalistic tradition, both Matthew and Luke lifted his copy. Much of what Mark wrote ended up in their accounts as well. Maybe they knew he was a reliable source.

But even Mark didn't get the scoop. According to Matthew's gospel, some other people got there first.

In thousands of school Nativity plays, watched by adoring parents and exhausted teachers, these characters appear as the Three Wise Men. Whether they were in real life kings, wise men, or some sort of astronomers or astrologers, we do not know. We don't even know that there were three of them, only that they are reported to have brought three different kinds of gifts.

They appear only once in the source documents of our faith, and that is in Matthew's gospel. Mark, Luke and John don't even mention them. One answer may be that Matthew was particularly keen to stress the link between the Christ person and the hopes and expectations to be found in the Old Testament. The appearance of the astrologers may have been for him a confirmation that these hopes and expectations were being fulfilled: the world drawing close to encounter the Word of God.

In one sense it doesn't matter very much who these characters were. They are not essential to the Christ event, but they are still significant for two reasons.

First, because they are part of the evidence that has been handed down to us, by Matthew and others in the persecuted early church. And that writing and handing on was a costly business. Just because some material does not seem helpful or convenient to us at a particular time is no reason for throwing it out. There are some parts of the gospel accounts which are both untidy and difficult. But life is untidy and difficult. It would be far more worrying if every bit agreed and the whole thing fitted neatly together like a jigsaw puzzle.

And, second, the story of the wise men is important because it holds up before us a profound truth: that we learn by journeying – and by encountering new and unexpected situations.

The wise men, says Matthew, came from the East. They journeyed from another place and another culture. And they journeyed into the unknown. Even today travel can be wearying and sometimes dangerous. In the ancient world it involved much more danger. The wise men had embarked on a high-risk venture which had no clear destination.

Did they all come from the same place? Did they plan the expedition together? Did they all set off at the same time in a convoy? Did one have a map? Were there such things as maps? Who paid for it all? Who did they leave behind to mind the shop? Would they ever return? Were they afraid?

Matthew says they were following a star, a new star which they had not seen before and which they could not therefore identify. Was it so clear in the sky that they all saw it, and all agreed on its significance?

Perhaps they came from different towns or different countries and met on the way, as travellers often do when they are making for a common destination. Were they drawn together by this one common purpose?

Did they fall out and argue about things on the way? Did they even speak the same language? In his wonderful poem about the Magi, or Wise Men, T. S. Eliot pictures them as having a very hard time; the route taking them over difficult terrain and their camels being obstinate and cantankerous.

What went through their minds on that journey? Travelling through an alien and unknown territory, fearing attack by robbers, sleeping rough as often as not, trying to control bloody-minded camels; and all the time wondering whether they had dreamt the whole ridiculous business.

What was it that drove them on? That depends a bit on who they were. If they were kings, it is difficult to see why they would bother to make the journey at all. If you are king, the last thing you need is another king being born and cluttering the place up. You might be declared redundant.

If they were astronomers, it might make a bit more sense. In the ancient world astronomers were, roughly speaking, what scientists are to us today. They were people who were concerned with finding out the truth: people who saw something new and wanted to know 'Why?'

It would be quite ironic if these three strangers were astronomers. For hundreds of years there has been a significant divide between people of science and people of faith. Scientists have tended to say that they are committed to the disciplined examination of reality, and that the others are at best dreamers and at worst fools and charlatans. The people of faith, however, have tended to claim that they, too, are exploring the truth, but that the scientists are missing out on a whole dimension of that reality.

To which group might those wise men have belonged? And what did they expect to find at the end of it all? A great king? A palace? A warm welcome and, just as important, warm beds?

What do we expect to find at the end of it all? A commercial computer-generated image of a jingle-bells Christmas? Or something else?

Like the wise men on their journeying, we may find the meaning of our Advent adventure is not what we expected. And, as we shall see tomorrow, neither is it safely locked away in the past.

18 DECEMBER

A mother's pain

————◆————

The scene is familiar. A young woman is giving birth to a child. She and her people live in a land ruled by oppression and fear. A foreign invader has overrun their country. Everywhere there is injustice and suffering. But, despite that, this is a time of rejoicing. The baby born this day is healthy and it is a boy.

Many will rejoice that he was born. He is destined to be great in the land. He will give his life seeking freedom for those in captivity and bringing good news to the poor. He will be a person of true compassion, expressed in a powerful sharing in the suffering of the people.

The mother does not know this as she holds him in her arms. Like all mothers before her, she wonders what the future will bring for her child. She does not know yet that he will be a sign that many will reject, and that a sword will enter her own heart also.

Who is this baby boy? We might be talking about the Christ-child or that strange figure, John the Baptist. But the child born exactly 50 years ago today is neither, although he will bring to his own world a passion for justice and a love of humanity found in both these people.

The child's name is Stephen Biko. He was born into a South Africa disfigured by the evil of apartheid, a beautiful country where greed had consigned the black population to slavery. Apartheid was a system of racial segregation created to legitimize cheap labour and to create fabulous wealth for its powerful white minority.

An intelligent boy, Steve Biko grew up in a poor family. Thanks to the hard work and dedication of his mother,

Alice, he was able to go to college to study to be a doctor. But the family's hopes for his success in medicine were to be dashed. As the political situation worsened in the early seventies, Biko abandoned his medical studies to join the non-violent Black Consciousness movement in South Africa.

The story of his life is as turbulent as the story of the nation into which he was born. He became a key national figure in the struggle for justice and played a vital part in helping his own people to rediscover their traditions and values. He opposed the idea that all concessions must be handed down as an act of charity by the reluctant whites, like crumbs from the rich man's table. The black person was a noble part of creation, independently of any reference to white culture.

Although he was part of a non-violent movement, Biko inevitably fell foul of the white power élite and on 7 September 1977 he was arrested by the South African police. In police custody he was tortured and subjected to severe beatings. As a result he suffered massive head injuries.

Three days later he was put in the back of a police Land Rover and driven, naked, for 700 miles from Port Elizabeth to Pretoria. Twenty-four hours later, on 12 September 1977, he died from his injuries. He was 30 years old.

The photographs of the mourners at Steve Biko's funeral show faces of silent, profound grief for a young life cut short by the forces of power and oppression, but perhaps also for the tragic inhumanity of a nation trapped in the evil of its rulers' own making. One picture shows his mother, his young wife, and their own young son. Who was it who broke the news to him and said: 'You will never see Daddy again'?

And, looking at that picture, we seem very close to another mother who was willing to let go of her child, even though a sword would enter her own heart also. A woman who stood at the foot of the cross and thought back to the moment when she had first held that small life in her arms and wondered what the future might bring.

Steve Biko was not a saint but he was almost certainly a martyr: a witness giving his life for the possibility of hope in the bloody tragedy of his nation.

In his struggle for truth and humanity he developed a deep faith in God, but a profound hostility to what he saw as the cold and cruel religion of the immigrant colonial church. He rejected the distorted image of the Christ person presented by the white European culture, and yet in his own life lived out the love of God. A close friend, the holy and wise monk Aelred Stubbs, a man not given to sentimentality, said on one occasion that life in Biko's company was like the Kingdom of God.

On the one hand, Biko had no option but to reject the Christianity of the whites. The entire structure of economic and spiritual oppression had been built on the premise that the black person was inferior. This, in its turn, had been born out of what Biko called the campaign of emotional terror inflicted on the black population by the waves of white Christian missionaries who had come to Africa centuries before.

What they assumed they had found were godless savages. What they in fact may have found, but failed to recognize, was a civilization able not only to worship God but to integrate that worship and spirituality into daily life, something the Western churches do not always achieve.

Biko's life was dedicated, not to violence, but to truth and justice. The truth was that the black person was a full and complete human being, and justice required that truth be lived out. He rejected the Western image of a passive God who allows injustice to go unchallenged; instead he believed in a God passionately concerned about the lives of the poor and oppressed.

Whether Biko ever read the Old Testament is not clear, but his life seems to have been a contemporary expression of much of what we find in Amos, Isaiah and the Psalms.

It is only by the coincidence of the date of his birth that his path crosses ours on our Advent journey. At first it seems to intrude into our exploration of what the Church calls the Incarnation – the Christ born among us. But, as we reflect on Steve Biko's birth in poverty, his life of care and compassion for the oppressed, his humour and vitality as a human being, and his death at the hands of the police, we cannot help being struck by the similarities with the story of Christ.

Another man who might have become a leader of his nation, beaten to death by the hatred of those in authority, who also claimed religious superiority.

'Are you the Christ? Are you the one who is to come?' John the Baptist had asked of Jesus. Locked away in his prison cell awaiting his own execution, John needed to know whether the hope of deliverance was still alive.

At one time John had himself been asked whether he was the Christ person. And what a temptation it must have been to say 'Yes'. But he was not. Neither was Steve Biko. But the power and love of Christ shone through in his young life also.

19 DECEMBER

Love and a muddy bucket

The curate was not having a good day. Apart from the fact that it had been raining for most of the past week, there was the small matter of the funeral. Someone had died 80 miles away in Hull. So, how come he had been landed with the funeral? Because the man and his wife had been married here.

How stupid, he thought, as he walked across to the church. The rain had stopped but the November afternoon was dank and gloomy. He walked round the church into the churchyard which covered most of the hillside. He needed to double-check where the grave was. It looked bad if you set off from the church with a coffin and a procession of mourners behind you, and then forgot where the grave was.

It was there, down towards the bottom of the hillside. Albert the grave-digger was some way off having a smoke under a tree. As the curate reached the grave he saw that there was a foot of water in the bottom. To dig a grave is to dig a well. He groaned and walked back up to the church which towered above him, its stonework blackened with a hundred years of industrial pollution.

Twenty-five minutes later the funeral arrived and out of the first large black limousine stepped one of the smallest old ladies he had ever seen. She looked very crumpled.

Instinctively he took her hand and said a few words. Then they walked up the long path to the church together. For the first time in more than 60 years she was back in the church where she had been married. He kept hold of her hand.

After the service the curate led the widow and the mourners on the long walk down to the graveside. He thought about the water in the grave and wondered whether the coffin would float. There was nothing he could do.

As they got nearer the grave, he saw the grave-digger suddenly scramble out of the hole and disappear behind a tree. What was the fool up to?

The undertaker helped the widow and the other mourners to step onto the wooden boards at the side of the grave. The boards were unsteady on the freshly dug earth and the curate found himself holding her hand again.

He looked down into the grave at the muddy water. But there was no water. It had all been baled out. Instead there was a covering of newly cut ferns. 'That's nice,' said the widow. 'Yes,' said the curate, looking round for the grave-digger, but there was no sign of him.

The coffin was lowered gently into the ground. The curate continued to hold the widow's hand as he said the prayers of committal. He could feel her shaking with grief. Sixty years before she had held another young man's hand. It seemed only yesterday. Now, only a few yards away from the place where they had been married, she was saying goodbye to him.

A little later the funeral cars disappeared round the bend in the lane and the curate never saw her again. The following week he received a letter written in an unsteady hand. It was from the widow, thanking him. In it were two crumpled one-pound notes.

Why had she brought her husband home to be buried? What did it matter? He could just as well have been buried in Hull. But it did matter. Bringing him home was a final act of loving.

It also had a huge and lasting effect on the curate. He would never forget her, and he had developed a new respect for grave-diggers. Albert never came to church, but baling out the grave and scattering the carpet of fresh ferns was a gesture as important as any sacrament.

As we are drawn closer to the Christmas event we need to ask: why was the Christ-child born at all? Surely God could have thought up some other way of saving the world. We could all have been genetically programmed to care for one another. If scientists can alter food genetically, then surely God can do the same with humans.

But he didn't. Whatever goes on in our food laboratories,

God doesn't operate in such a cost-effective way. As he made them, human beings require the experience of human interaction. We learn life's deepest truths only through our experience of the physical.

It was physically seeing his servant at the point of death that made the centurion ask for the Christ person's help. And it was in the physical silence of waiting for him to arrive that the realization of who Jesus was burst upon him.

Perhaps that's why, a few years later, when Jesus was trying to communicate to his thick-headed friends just what his friendship with them was all about, he used a loaf of bread and a jug of wine.

Instead of a three-hour debate on The Mystery of Salvation, he tore up the bread and handed it to them. 'This is my body,' he said, 'given for you. Eat it.' Then he took the wine and said: 'This wine is my life, poured out for you. Drink it, all of you.'

They ate the bread and drank the wine. They almost certainly didn't understand what was going on. But they did not forget what had happened.

Perhaps that's why, in John's majestic gospel, when the Christ person wanted them to understand the meaning of the word 'love', he got a bowl of water, rolled up his sleeves and washed their mucky feet. Crude but effective. They never again needed to ask what love meant, or what their calling was.

Perhaps that's why God brought a little old lady all the way from Hull that gloomy afternoon. There was a thick-headed curate who needed to discover what the word 'ministry' meant. And a grave-digger with a muddy bucket to show him what a sacrament was. An outward and visible sign of an inward grace.

Perhaps that's why God said to a girl called Mary: 'Help me. Help me to show this dim-witted world what it means to have life.' And, as she held that child in her womb, did she also say: 'This is my body, my own being, given for you'?

Perhaps, at the end of the day, buckets and blood and bodies and bread are all that we can truly understand. And maybe that's how God wants it to be. Maybe that's the way he made us.

20 DECEMBER

Death on the doorstep

The murder of the Liverpool vicar, Christopher Grey, touched a nerve among a vast number of people in Britain, much as the Dunblane massacre had done only a few months earlier.

It was not simply that someone had been murdered – that happens every day of the year. It was more a matter of an innocent life with huge potential being wasted in such a needless and senseless way. A person who had dedicated his life to the service of a materially deprived area was suddenly dying on his own vicarage doorstep.

The first reports of the tragedy came as a personal shock. A very dear friend is a vicar in that part of Liverpool and for the first few hours I thought that he had been killed. I rang him repeatedly but there was no reply from the vicarage. I didn't know that he was away on holiday or that there were two parishes in that area of the city.

Only later did I discover that Peter was alive and that it was Chris, his neighbouring colleague, who was dead.

The tragedy highlighted the harshness of life in Britain's inner cities, a harshness often imposed on damaged and impoverished communities from outside by an unjust system of values.

It made me reflect on the homeless people I know and the impoverished community just down the road from where I live. As in all of society, a few of these people may be just plain evil, but the vast majority seem to be the same fallible bundle of virtues and vices that the rest of us are.

The difference is that they are not treated like the rest of us. Whether by the tabloid press or by tabloid politicians, people in these areas are often treated with dehumanizing contempt.

But they are human like the rest of us. As Shylock the Jew cried out to his Christian tormentors: 'If you prick us, do we not bleed?' So, too, the people of our inner cities bleed, but we do not hear their cry of pain. Uneasy at our own complicity in the situation, we distance ourselves from the pain in case we too are touched by the suffering and the despair.

Shylock reacted with anger and frustration against injustice. He was only a fictional character, but did he reflect a reality which Shakespeare had seen in real life? In our own communities people react with similar frustration, and sometimes with anger, to situations of unemployment, racism and homelessness. Often those who hit the headlines are people in need of psychiatric help, and when that help is not accessible things can go disastrously wrong.

But these are not actors in a play, they are people in real life. So, too, the people we meet on our Advent journey are people from real life.

The tragedy is that the people and events we encounter in Luke's gospel are intended to be a sign of hope for a damaged world. The fact that the Christ-child is to be born at all is a profound statement about God's involvement and caring for creation. Religion always seems to want to distance what it calls 'the spiritual' from the earthly, following the ancient Greek idea that the spiritual is pure and free, while the material is base, unclean and imprisoning.

But, in the gospels, from the outset we see this false barrier being broken down. Birth is a messy business and, whichever way you look at it, the Christian faith begins with a birth. Whether or not the mother of the Christ-child was a virgin and whether we have got the date quite right, we shall probably never know. And it may be that neither matters. But what is beyond all doubt is that the person we know as Jesus Christ was physically born.

The fact of his birth is profoundly important, not least because it fits in with the manner and the message of his life. In all the bustle and excitement of Christmas shopping, carol services and school Nativity plays, the birth event seems to have become detached from the rest of the Christ story.

The coming New Year celebrations will not only mark the end of the old year, they will also effectively close off the Christmas event for another 12 months. We put away the Christmas story with the Christmas decorations, and both seem significantly past their sell-by date.

That is a very convenient way for us to deal with a challenging and disturbing event, but it is not true to the facts. The facts are that the Christmas story is an ongoing event with highly threatening social and economic implications.

If the Christ event is basically true, and if John in his radically different gospel is right in saying that it came about because of God's love for our unclean little world, then we have an awkward situation developing here. Because, if all this is consistent with the words and actions of the Christ person, not only is God concerned with physical and worldly matters, but we are being drawn into this mess too.

Some traditionalists say the Church should not get involved in economics and politics. They say that religion is for Sundays only, and that spirituality is about the 'higher' things. But God seems to be saying just the opposite.

But how can we dare to suggest what God is saying? Only by looking at the words and actions of Jesus Christ, whom the Church believes to be the human expression of the will and purpose of God himself. And what do we see Jesus doing?

We see him being born in the filth of a stable and growing up to befriend the unwashed and the outcast. We see him touch with passionate compassion the defiled and defiling leper. We see him eating and drinking with the cheats and the harlots, and grovelling in the dust, mixing his spittle with dirt to heal the blind. We see him, touched by a prostitute, declare her action a blessing that will be remembered for all time.

Why is all this going on, when we are all supposed to be pure and spiritual? Because this is what the word 'love' is all about, if it is real love and involves real people.

It comes as no surprise to think that Christopher Grey was loved by God. As a dedicated follower of the Christ person, it is natural that he should be loved by God. But it comes as a profound shock to realize that the person who murdered him is also loved by God. Both were – and are – precious to the one who made them.

But, if that is true, what of our own relationship with these people? Are we not called to love both the priest and the person of violence in the inner city? What if the people we see portrayed in our newspapers as the undeserving poor are in fact children of God, as we are ourselves? And, if children of God, our own sisters and brothers too?

These are not sub-human animals to be chained up, but people who are often damaged by our own greed and indifference. They are people who suffer the consequences of our own economic and political decisions and acts of self-interest. The way we vote is a spiritual action: it speaks of and influences the way we relate to our neighbour, and to the God who loves that neighbour.

The festival of Christmas which celebrates the involvement of God in the material world is intended to be a sign of hope and life, expressed to real people through material things such as a house to live in and food to eat.

How ironic that it should have become for most people an excuse for greed and self-indulgence. Instead of drawing us together in a common bond of caring and love, it is as though it divides us into two opposing groups: the rich who have and the poor who have not; those inside in the warm and brightly lit shops and those who can only stand outside in the cold.

The problem is that, as we do our final round of Christmas shopping, we hear through the sound of carols an echo of another time when someone said: 'I was hungry and you did not feed me; I was naked and you did not clothe me.' He will divide the people into two groups, Matthew tells us. And we wonder whether Christmas is the beginning or the end.

21 DECEMBER
The final approach

―◆―

Inside the aircraft it is warm and bright. The cabin crew are clearing away the last of the food trays. Above us on the television screens the in-flight video is coming to an end. Outside it is dark. We have no way of knowing exactly where we are, but we know we are nearing the end of our journey.

The pilot's voice comes over the intercom: 'We shall shortly be starting our descent. Please return to your seats.' Almost immediately the nose of the aircraft begins to dip and we can feel ourselves starting to lose height. We have begun our final approach.

Below us several miles ahead in the darkness is the runway. There is the slightest hint of anxiety as we wonder how the pilot will find the exact flight path to bring us down safely.

Even after all these centuries, travel is still uncertain. On our Advent journey we too have begun our final approach, but to what destination and with whom? Who are the people travelling with us? Aboard the plane we realize that we are not in control of our own lives. Someone else is flying the aircraft and it is too late to turn back.

In another place a young woman knows that she is no longer in control of her own life, and that it is too late to turn back. The child in her womb is moving and will soon be born. She too is on her final approach.

The man at her side is deeply worried. He has faith, but that faith is falling short at the moment. Disaster is the word that keeps coming to mind. Not only is the woman to whom he is betrothed about to have a child, they are also being forced to make a quite unnecessary trek from one end of the country to the other.

The Roman authorities have announced a census and they are required to return to the home town of their family. It happens every 14 years. He should have remembered, but he hadn't. What difference would it have made anyway?

The straight-line distance is about 75 miles, but they are not aboard an aircraft and they are not travelling in a straight line. To make the 100-mile journey at this time of year and in the advanced stages of pregnancy is madness. It will almost certainly end in disaster.

Meanwhile, as we are aware, other people are making a journey into the unknown. Three men, unsure of what they are doing or where they are, continue their bizarre expedition. Is there a star? Is it a new star? Is it the same star they saw yesterday? Suddenly all the stars look alike.

They are travelling through unknown and alien territory. People treat them with suspicion, sometimes with open hostility. And the bloody-minded camels seem to sense that all is not well. Perhaps they, too, know that this could end in disaster.

But it is too late to turn back now. What would people say? That they had given up with the end in sight? That they had changed their minds? That they weren't so wise and clever after all? Tired and footsore, they must be coming close to the end. All their lives they have been well-organized and disciplined, and they have been respected as people of wisdom and learning. 'Trust me, I'm a wise man.' But for some time now they have had the feeling that they no longer know anything.

Adrift in a strange land, they are vulnerable. They too are making their final approach. But what is their destination and what is it that awaits them? There are no runway lights. They are flying blind.

On the night of 17 March 1941, 11 Wellington bombers took off from RAF Mildenhall in Suffolk for a raid over Bremen in Germany. Losses had been high in the squadron over the past few months and aboard the aircraft flying in formation above the clouds the young crewmen, some still in their teens, were uneasy.

It was a long flight, but they had reached their target and dropped their cargo of bombs. Where exactly, they did not know. Then they had started the slow journey home to safety.

Aboard one of the Wellingtons, the crew were looking forward to a well-earned rest from flying. Dawn was breaking as they crossed the Channel and they must have breathed a sigh of relief as they began their final approach to the airfield.

They did not know it, but they had only minutes to live. Above them, in the clouds, was an enemy fighter. As they came in to land, the Wellington was raked with machine-gun fire. The pilot was killed instantly and the plane went out of control, over-shooting the runway and crashing onto a bungalow. There were no survivors.

At the end of their long and hazardous journey they had thought that they were safe. They could see their destination and the landing lights guiding them home. They could almost feel the reassuring jolt of the huge bomber touching down. Within minutes they would be back in the squadron canteen. Then: disaster.

What is waiting for our travellers as they make their final approach? They carry no bombs, but their journey is, in a strange way, destined for the destruction of a whole way of life. There will be people who will not welcome their arrival and will resist the threat of change ruthlessly.

Meanwhile, the young woman can feel the first spasms of pain in her own body. Faith is not without risk. Within a few days she will experience the pain of birth. But what after that?

Is she so utterly confident that she feels no sense of unease or fear in these last few days? Do the words of the Magnificat ringing in her ears block out the doubts and the questions? Or does she sometimes find herself suddenly gripped by panic and pray in desperation: 'Lord, take this cup away from me'?

22 DECEMBER
The best-laid plans . . .

———◆———

It's odd how even the most carefully made plans can go haywire at the very last moment. Some years ago there was a bishop, dearly loved for his crusty sense of humour and refreshing dislike of pomposity.

One day he came to conduct a confirmation service at a rather up-market suburban church. The vicar had made quite sure that everything was ready. Two minutes before the service was due to begin, the impressively large choir formed up and his lordship said the vestry prayer. Dead on time, the choir vestry door was opened onto the packed church and the organist struck up with the first rousing hymn.

Slowly and with great solemnity, like a great railway train from the days of steam, the choir led off – up the side aisle to the back of the church – before turning to process back down the centre aisle towards the high altar.

Traditionally the choir walk in front, led by the cross-bearer, and the clergy follow with the most senior person coming last. Six foot two in his socks, the bishop, an ex-Army chaplain mentioned in dispatches, looked magnificent in cope and mitre.

Smiling with approval as he watched the choir move away, the bishop pulled the vestry door briskly shut behind him. He heard the latch drop as he turned to follow the procession.

But then it all started to go wrong. His robe had caught in the vestry door and the door had locked behind him. He turned to call out to the vicar, but he was now some way down the side aisle. The choir and organist were giving of their best and his words were drowned out by the singing. He was a prisoner.

He watched helplessly as the procession moved relentlessly round the church, leaving the bishop marooned far behind. Eventually the vicar realized that the bishop was not where he ought to be and an embarrassing rescue operation was launched. Organists who can improvise in such a situation while all around them are losing their composure are a treasure beyond price.

Whether it is confirmations or Christmas, the best-laid plans can go wrong. And, considering how many thousands of years people have been having babies, and how much warning we get of their arrival, it's strange that we don't always get that right either.

That being so, there is something grimly familiar about the way in which the Christ-child was born. Having survived the 100-mile journey to the family's home town, the young woman and her betrothed husband apparently found the place in chaos.

Hundreds, if not thousands, of people had been forced to travel to other parts of the country to register in the census. As a result, lodgings were at a premium. Luke describes the situation briefly, but his familiar words reveal a situation that might quickly turn into a disaster: 'While they were there the time came for her baby to be born. She gave birth to her son, her first-born ... she laid him in a manger, because there was no room for them to lodge in the house' (Luke 2:6, 7).

There was no room? This was a young woman about to give birth, and there was no room? We have to be very careful about constructing imaginary scenes and making up imaginary conversations: it is all too easy to move into the world of make-believe.

On the other hand, without giving further thought to how people might feel and react in such crisis situations, we are in danger of losing much of the power and meaning of what is going on.

It may not be entirely true that money can buy you anything, but one suspects it can buy you hotel accommodation if you can pay the price. But apparently the parents of the

Christ-child couldn't pay the price. Neither, it seems, were they regarded as sufficiently important people for a room to be found. Perhaps, after all those days on the road, they did not look very clean.

Imagine the stress for both Mary and her husband as they realized that no one would take them in. Imagine how they might have felt as they realized that the baby was about to be born into this chaotic situation.

Were they not angry that no one would give them lodgings? Were they not in despair as the birth pains increased and they desperately looked for some place of shelter? Were they not asking where God was in all this? For, if this was a child of God, then why was God not managing things better?

Or didn't they have feelings like that? Were they plaster images, gliding through this nativity drama in a glow of religious rapture? Is this a religious pantomime being enacted with no reference to real life, and therefore with no real contact point for us as ordinary human beings? Or is this an authentic, though perhaps inadequate, description of a real-life situation? We need to know what we are dealing with.

Either this is God, the source of all meaning and reality, interacting with the physical world in which mortal people live, lust, work, worry and die, or it is nothing.

The problem is that many people, especially those who have power, want God to be narrowly religious. And the fact is that he may not be. In later years the holy people and those in positions of power were to attack the Christ person for not being religious enough; that is, for not being sufficiently pious and other-worldly. And what was his reaction to that criticism? He was furious.

He told them: 'John the Baptist came, living a life of monastic simplicity and never touching a drink, and you all said he was mad. Now here is the Son of Man, both eating and drinking, and you call him a glutton and drunkard.'

There is plenty of frustration and anger in those words. Perhaps feelings were running similarly high in the hours before that 'glutton and drunkard' was born.

23 DECEMBER
Leaves on the line

——◆——

Imagine for a moment that the Queen is travelling to Balmoral in Scotland on the Royal Train. As she passes through Leeds, the engine suddenly fails, or there are leaves on the line, and she is forced to break her journey. The Lord Lieutenant is called out and an equerry is sent to arrange a suite of rooms at the best hotel.

Unfortunately there is a big conference taking place in the city and that particular night there are no rooms. Nowhere in the entire city is there a spare room. Is the Queen going to spend the night on a bench on Platform 5 of Leeds City Station? No. Someone who is staying in a room at the best hotel is going to be moved out. When you have power, status and wealth, doors open. People do not say no to you.

So it seems clear that the Christ-child is born of parents who have very little in the way of power, wealth and status. And when people are without those things, people tend to say 'No' very often, as homeless people will tell you.

The conversations between the parents of the Christ-child and the different hotel and lodging-house keepers may not have been so very different from the conversations between homeless families and bed-and-breakfast proprietors in any city in any wealthy industrialized nation this Christmas.

Christmas, despite all the hopes and expectations, can be a very divisive time of year. It divides the haves from the have-nots, the 'Yes, of course we have a room for you' people from the 'No, we haven't any vacancies – push off' people. It is the time of year when many families come together because that is what they are expected to do, only to discover they are not very happy families. And even the £7 billion we have

84

just spent on presents and drink this Christmas isn't enough to paper over those domestic cracks.

Ironically, Christmas is a time of increased loneliness and despair, for the simple reason that we are expected to be happy and festive. People are led to believe that everyone else is wonderfully happy, and their own despair is made the harder to bear.

Ironically, too, the churches are in danger of colluding with this situation. At every single church in this country there are good and loving people worshipping God and sincerely trying to express the wonder of what Christmas means. But, even though the intention is good and honest, there are times when the outcome can be damaging for many other people.

Perhaps, just for once, all the churches could declare an amnesty and cancel all their Christmas festivities. Perhaps they could hold services of utter simplicity in unheated buildings as a sign of solidarity, not only with the poor, but with the original Christmas birth.

Perhaps if the churches pulled the plug on all the hype and stereotyping of Christmas, we might discover a new meaning – or maybe the original meaning. It might even be a prophetic sign for the politicians to change their priorities, which are only our priorities anyway.

What a miracle it would be if we could spend our £7 billion of Christmas cash on homes for other people. How many decent houses would that buy? This year the building societies are giving away £30 billion in bonuses to their lenders. Do we really need all that money? What could we do for homeless people with £37 billion?

On the boxes of free-range eggs we get from the supermarket, it says the eggs come from hens that are free to roam, perch, poke around for corn in the dust, and not to have to worry about being eaten by foxes. Houses need to provide that sort of freedom and security for people.

Instead, thousands of children exist like battery hens in damp, cold, crowded accommodation where whole families are forced to live in a single room. They do not have the space to grow and, like hens on factory farms, they peck each other and themselves. Their environment encourages physical and mental illness, bed-wetting and socially disruptive behaviour.

Over the past 15 to 20 years the poor have been getting poorer in real terms and the rich have been getting very much richer. The wealth of the top income group has risen so much that it has pulled the whole national average income upwards. Yes, as a nation we have on average become richer. But only because those at the top have creamed off so much of the wealth. Those at the bottom are poorer: nothing has trickled down except despair.

Forty-eight hours before Christmas Day these are not just politically sensitive statistics. They are part of the reality of our neighbours' lives. They are part of our relationship with God. They have a meaning and an implication that is at the heart of our faith and spirituality. They are also part of Christmas itself, for if we are true to Luke's account of what happened we find the Christ-child himself now homeless and rejected by his own people. His own unmarried parents are apparently too poor to buy their way into even the most basic hotel for the night.

This is the child of whom choirs in every cathedral in the land will sing, and the congregations will come largely from the middle- and upper-income groups. There will be few homeless people among those congregations. And yet they will expect the homeless Christ-child to be there, the one who was to say: 'I have come to proclaim good news to the poor.' And to pay the price of that statement with his life.

If the Christ person was saying 2,000 years ago that he is the homeless and the naked, is he not still saying it today? And if he is saying it today in our own towns and cities, then where is it that we shall encounter him this Christmas? At the best hotel in town or on a bench on Platform 5 of Leeds City Station?

24 DECEMBER

Unexpected visitors

———◆———

Why did he do it? Why did he all but ruin a good story? Luke's gospel begins with some of the finest Greek in the whole of the New Testament. He is writing to a high-ranking Roman official, and to the entire Gentile world. Unlike the three other gospel writers, Luke is himself a Gentile. An advocate from the Gentile world speaking to the Gentile world.

His message has been carefully researched both from eye-witnesses and from written texts which he judges trustworthy. His message is for him the most important communication in the world. He is a cultured man writing to the social and political élite on matters of the deepest significance. A lot hangs on what he is about to say.

His account begins with the dramatic and moving account of the birth of a child to the elderly and barren woman Elizabeth as a symbol of the loving power of God. Then the discovery of Mary that she will conceive the Christ-child evokes from her the powerful and prophetic words we call the Magnificat.

Zechariah, the father of John the Baptist, himself speaks the majestic words of the Benedictus:

You, child, will be called the prophet of the Most High; for you will go before the Lord to prepare his ways; to give knowledge of salvation to his people in the forgive-ness of their sins, through the tender mercy of our God, when the day shall dawn upon us from on high to give light to those who sit in darkness and in the shadow of death, and to guide our feet into the way of peace.

(Luke 1:76–9, RSV)

For the first couple of pages of his gospel, Luke is looking good. The vision, the imagery and the language are power-ful and noble. The drama moves forward with increasing expectation. And then what do we find?

Shepherds.

Who cares about shepherds? What have shepherds to do with anything? At this critical moment, the birth of the Christ, the Son of the Most High, Luke appears to throw it all away. He presents us with a ridiculous image of a bunch of shepherds on a hillside being confronted by the angel of the Lord. And alongside this angel of the Lord, says Luke the cultured Gentile, is a 'multitude of angels – the heavenly host'. Quite an encounter, but not one likely to impress a sophisticated readership.

Things are rapidly going from bad to worse for Luke. What is the message of this angel of the Lord? That the saviour of the world has been born. And where is this very important child to be found? In a cowshed.

Surely Marx was right and religion is the opium of the people. Mindless ritual blunts our senses, takes away the pain of life, and stops us asking questions. But the Christ event is not about religion; it is about life. Why is it that at this point on our important journey of faith we are confronted by a ragged bunch of shepherds? Who are these people and why have they suddenly intruded into our story?

Admittedly, shepherds had an important role in life. They kept alive and edible the food supply. Traditionally God was pictured as the Great Shepherd, guiding and often disciplining his people. But the day-to-day reality was somewhat less attractive.

The shepherds who lived a very basic existence on the hillsides had no way, and probably little inclination, to keep the religious laws. They did not pray at the required times of the day and they were not supplied with shower and toilet facilities. They were often regarded as unclean and sinful. Chaucer's picturesque image of the 'shitten shepherd' comes to mind. So what do we get from Luke? A grubby bunch of outcasts confronted by the massed angelic hosts of heaven.

And what does the big angel say? Not 'Please direct me to

your king, I have important news for the world.' According
to Luke he or she says: 'I bring *you* good news. Today is born
to *you* a saviour.' (Considering that the shepherds are an
appalling and irrelevant intrusion into this whole scenario,
there is a lot of direct-quotes dialogue going on here.)

Is Luke mad? Judging by the rest of his gospel, he is not.
He is an intelligent writer who has suddenly made a dis-
covery. Think for a moment about what has been going on.
Luke is by all accounts a friend and companion of St Paul.
In the past few years other people have written accounts of
the Christ event but, with the exception of St Mark's account,
Luke does not seem very impressed.

He wants to explore this case himself; to test out for himself the validity of what is being said; and to write his own
careful account of what happened. And so, using material he
has collected for the past few years, he starts his own gospel.
But he does not begin at chapter one. He begins at what we
now call chapter three. Take a look for yourself.

As he begins his task he is on the outside, looking in. He
writes using at least three clear sources: Mark's gospel, of
which he uses about half; a source called 'Q', which both he
and St Matthew use; and the source called 'L', which is
unique to Luke himself. But as he writes something happens:
he gets caught up in the story – which changes in tempo.

The first couple of chapters are measured and steady, but
at chapter six we move up a gear. And as the gospel moves
forward, there is a change of mood. There is challenge and
warning, and the first hint of anger. Then open conflict
breaks out and there is the looming fear of death.

Almost unnoticed, Luke is picking up speed. The momen-
tum and power build as the drama mounts: the mystery of
the Last Supper and the anguish of Gethsemane; the betrayal
by Peter and the desolation and abandonment of the Cross.
The strange exchange of words with the unrepentant thief
on the cross who at the moment of death seems to affirm
Jesus as the Christ. Hurtling forward into the Resurrection
account, Luke tries to end the gospel with the final parting
of the Christ person, but he is travelling too fast.

No wonder he went on to write the book called the Acts of the Apostles. But before that, he has something else to do. He goes back and writes the introduction to his gospel. With all the power and conviction of the Crucifixion and Resurrection ringing in his ears, he writes to his 'Most Excellent Theophilus'.

When do you write the introduction to a book? At the end when you have written the rest of it. Why wait until then? Because, until then, you do not know whether there is anything worth writing an introduction for. Luke now knows that there is.

But why shepherds? Because only after hearing the gospel, reliving the gospel and, finally, writing down the gospel, does he suddenly realize their significance.

The Gospel, Luke has discovered, is the good news of life for the poor: for the unclean and the outcast. Suddenly this shepherd story, which Mary has been treasuring in her heart, makes sense. Suddenly the stable becomes a cathedral and the first act of Christian worship is attended not by popes and archbishops but by a bunch of ragged shepherds.

At that moment it is they who are the carriers of the good news. It is they who speak the Gospel words. It is they, the unlettered and the inarticulate, who tell the mother what they have themselves been told concerning the Christ-child. The Gospel is not only good news for the poor: it is good news from among the poor.

Why shepherds on this Christmas Eve? Because, as he completed his gospel and reflected on what it all meant, perhaps Luke saw the deep significance of these unwashed sinners from the hills. Far from being an intrusion in the gospel drama, they are an image of what the whole Christ event is about.

This strange Christ person's whole life was spent among the poor and the outcast. They were there in the pain and the chaos of his birth, and they were there, dying beside him, in the pain and the filth of his death.

Luke may be in danger of ruining our Christmas, but only by struggling to show us its real meaning.

25 DECEMBER
The gift of life

———◆———

Christmas Day has dawned. Indoors it is warm, a time for presents and celebration. Outside, the city streets are empty. No buses will be running today and many people without cars will not be able to meet with friends and families. Unless they can afford a taxi at Christmas rates, they will be stranded in their own homes.

The High Street shops are shut. In their windows bright red January Sales signs have appeared, but for the next 24 hours there will be an armistice in the sales war.

At the day centre, people who are homeless gather for their annual Christmas dinner. They are in many respects a great family of people: most of them know each other, although there are a number of younger, less familiar faces this year.

The dining-room is unusually full and, unlike other days of the year, everyone will eat at the same time. Because the room is crowded with extra tables and chairs, people cannot move around freely and there is a faint hint of institutionalism in the air. Not much different to millions of other families drawn together in the artificiality of the Great British Christmas Day.

Turkey, potatoes and veg are served with warm gravy on unstable paper plates and there are plastic knives and forks. Before the first course has been fully served some people are asking about the pudding, or for a glass of water. A few arrive late, having walked in from the outskirts of the city, and there is a moment of confusion as they are squeezed into the already packed dining-room.

At the end of the meal there is a video and, three hours

later as they finally leave, the guests are given a carrier-bag of food and a present in Christmas wrapping-paper.

It has been a strange gathering. In a way it has not been real. These were not cattle being fed, these were ordinary people with too little room for normal human contact, acutely aware that this is not how they would ideally have liked to spend Christmas Day. It has brought back pain and memories of loss and failure. But it was the best the day centre could do. It was not perfection, but it was done with love.

Years ago, on another Christmas morning, an immature young curate caused havoc in his church by preaching about 'the blood, the after-birth and the shit' of the stable. After the service a large woman in a fur coat stormed up the aisle and bellowed at him: 'How dare you ruin our Christmas with that sort of talk?'

How indeed? And how dare Luke ruin all our Christmases by expecting us to hear his words and dare to risk that they may be true?

Perhaps the curate's ill-chosen words were not appropriate for that Sung Eucharist. But the Christ-child was not born in a centrally heated suburban church. On that day the only fur coats were being worn by their original owners and the congregation was a handful of shepherds.

But maybe that wasn't such a bad thing after all: shepherds would have been well acquainted with the mess and the danger of birth. Employed to be both security guards and midwives, they protected their valuable sheep from attack from wild animals, and in the lambing season would often be up to their elbows in blood and after-birth. Perhaps they were useful people to have around when the Christ-child was being born. And with what irony was he later to be called the Lamb of God.

They were men of work, and the Christ-child's mother had been at work too. The work of birth is hard and, in the unhygienic surroundings of a cowshed, dangerous.

And were there gifts? There was the gift of a child to a young peasant girl. There was the gift of survival to the child itself – and the gift of relief to the bemused and distraught father hovering in the background.

There was the gift of the shepherds who carried with them the message of the angel, words not spoken and then forgotten, for the mother kept all these things and treasured them in her heart. Sixty years from now Luke will need to ask how we know that these things happened. 'The mother remembered these things,' he says.

And so it is that in the filth of the stable we see God reaching out in love to the undeserving world of High Street shopping and fashion-conscious greed. It is not in the cool, clean serenity of a cathedral that this momentous event takes place, but in a stable, echoing the Christ person's action in reaching out to the defiled and defiling leper; echoing the rashness of the father running to embrace the defiled and defiling prodigal son. As Ruth Rann has said, after that birth no one can make the excuse that they are not good enough or clean enough to receive the gift of God's love.

So, as they walk away from the day centre with their bags of groceries, past the newly opened branch of Harvey Nichols and the other glittering city shops, going who knows where, it seems that the only people who have no gift to give today are the homeless and unsettled of this city. The final condemnation in a productivity-oriented society is to have nothing to offer.

And yet there was a gift, one gift among many from these beloved people whom we assume have nothing, and are nothing and will always be nothing.

Some time ago a strange thing happened. There is a befriending group for people who are homeless or who live very unsettled lives. There are cups of tea, dominoes, darts, snooker, table tennis, and a short meeting where everybody shares in the planning of events and the running of the group. Sometimes they take themselves off on short holidays and twice a year they run a market stall of bric-a-brac and items such as bird feeders, calendars and icons which members make in a weekly workshop.

Last year the treasurer of this little group announced a

financial surplus. After taking out the rent for their room and paying other running costs, they had a couple of hundred pounds left. What should be done with it? Would it be spent on a big party or on packets of cigarettes for everybody? Would they buy warm clothing to see them through the coming winter?

No. They were of one mind: the money should be divided between the two hospices in the city. But not equally divided. One hospice, it was felt, always seemed to get more publicity than the other. It was therefore agreed that the larger share should go to the less well-known hospice.

There was no fuss or argument, and no sense of pride or self-satisfaction. Just a simple act of loving by people who often live close to death to others also living close to death.

A priest who is a member of the group sat through the discussion feeling increasingly thoughtful. For several years, his well-heeled church had congratulated itself on giving away 10 per cent of its income. This money had also been given in love, but never once did its generosity remotely endanger the comfortable security of the church.

Meanwhile, this small group, who were among the materially poorest people in the city, had just agreed to give away almost all that they had. Which group was living out the gospel? the priest asked himself. And in which group did he feel closer to the Risen Christ?

In the night-shelters and the hostels, sleeping under bridges and in rubbish skips, existing in bedsits often unfit for human habitation, hidden away from our disapproving gift-wrapped society, there live people who, though they have nothing, are somehow able to give everything.

No wonder the Christ-child born today spent so much of his life among them. Perhaps he too needed their generous love, thought the priest.

26 DECEMBER

The little frog

———◆———

Once upon a time there was a beautiful princess who loved to walk in the palace gardens. One morning as she walked with her maid and her page-boy they came to the lily pond. And there in the grass at her feet sat a small green frog.

'Keep away. It might jump,' said the maid. 'Hit it with a stick. Kill it,' said the page-boy. But the princess did neither. To their horror, she picked up the frog and, holding it gently in her hands, she kissed it. Suddenly, says the fairy story, the frog was changed into a handsome prince. And he and the princess were married and lived happily ever after.

Jesus was a frog. Not a real frog, but a frog person. He was someone looked down on by the rich and the powerful. To them he looked common but, worst of all, they never knew which way he was going to jump.

The reaction of the rich and powerful to this real-life frog person was exactly the same as that of the page-boy in the fairy story: they wanted to hit him with sticks and kill him. And that's what happened. But it wasn't the end of the story. After the frog person had been hit with sticks and nailed to a cross to die, it was as though God reached down and lifted this small creature up into new life.

When we read the gospels, we begin to realize what froggy gospels they are, because this frog person turns out to have a lot of very froggy friends. They were called sinners and prostitutes, publicans and outcasts. They were people who were looked down on by the respectable rich and powerful – and by many religious people.

But the Christ person loved his froggy friends and had a great respect and compassion for them. And he felt a blazing anger when they were hit with sticks, condemned as failures, rejected as being unclean, or shut out of the friendship of the community because they were ill or confused.

The frog person got into enormous trouble because he insisted that God loved frogs. He said that he had come to bring good news of life and hope to all the little frog people, because God had a special love for them.

No wonder the rich and the powerful people with the sticks got angry. If anyone could be loved by God, where did that leave them? 'Ah,' said the frog person, 'but you have had your reward already.'

Back in the cattle shed, our little frog is just one day old. The froggy shepherds have been and gone, leaving behind only their strange story of angels. Was it a vision or was it a dream? Is it a dream which wakes the mother of the little frog with a sudden feeling of unease? What is happening and why? Who is this child and what will he become? His birth in this cattle shed has so nearly brought death to them both. They have survived, for the time being, but death is near at hand.

A few miles away a new danger is beginning to emerge. Three strange travellers have arrived. Following a star they saw – or dreamed they saw – they have come close to the end of their journey.

But, while the angels came to the ragged shepherds on the hillsides, the three travellers have gone to the man at the top. Intelligent they may have been; wise they were not. 'A new king has been born,' they say. 'And we have followed his star. We have come to pay him homage.'

Just what every ruler least welcomes: competition. But the king is intelligent and diplomatic. 'Go and find this new king,' he says, 'and when you have found him, come and tell me where he is so that I too can go and worship him.' As he says this, he is fingering his sword.

Well fed and flattered by the king's smooth words, the three unwise men set off to find the little frog. According to Matthew, they carry gifts. But the invisible gift they carry is death. The trap is set. When the unwise men return to the king the trap will be sprung – and this little frog will no longer be a threat to national security.

However, Matthew tells us that the three travellers decided not to return to the king because they had a warning in a dream. Instead they went home by another route. Possibly. Or perhaps when they heard what was going on, Joseph and a couple of shepherds took them round the back of the stable and told them a few home truths. Some dream.

Powerful people do not happen on power by chance. They achieve power by single-minded dedication and the ruthless removal of opposition. Vested interests, whether economic, political or religious, are to be defended at all costs. It would not have taken the king long to realize that the three strangers were not coming back. Other arrangements would have to be made to deal with this little local difficulty.

Today, economic and political vested interests are guarded jealously. Multinational company profits are sacred. And if in the process a few people down at the bottom of the heap have to be silenced and the overseas aid budget slips to a new low, who cares? The Christ person says that God cares, and that, just as the princess married the frog, so it will be the frog people who will receive the love of God. But that Christ person would say that, wouldn't he? He was just another of those unpleasant little frog people himself.

Meanwhile the three unwise men prepared to set off for home. Who were they? Kings? Astronomers? Astrologers? Wise men? People versed in the secrets of the stars and able to discern signs and meanings hidden to ordinary people – and totally invisible to frogs?

Once again we find ourselves in an uncomfortable predicament: the experts, the people of worldly and religious authority, are somehow on the wrong side of the fence. And we have an unsettling suspicion that the people being called by God to bring hope and life to the world may be the poor, the unclean and the outcast.

The frog people.

A *night* to remember

————◆————

They say that climbing down a mountain can be even more difficult than climbing up it. Maybe the three unwise strangers found their journey home just as hard as it had been when they had a star to follow.

What did they say to themselves on that return journey? Were they glad and full of excitement at what they had found, or were they bitterly disappointed that it was only a baby in a cattle shed, a frog when they had expected a prince? And what had been the effect of their discovery, that simple encounter with the Christ-child? Experience is a great teacher; sometimes it's surprising what we learn.

It was a bit like that the night that seven clergymen slept together. They slept in cardboard boxes on the pavement outside the local Co-op department store. It was the night before the Churches National Housing Coalition lobby of Parliament. They could not get down to London to take part, so they had decided that, as an act of solidarity, they would stage a sleep-out in their own town.

It was a chilly December night but they were well prepared with thermal underwear and thick pullovers. At ten o'clock kindly church members brought them coffee and pizzas. Then, rather self-consciously, they bedded down for the night.

The wind made the steel shutters on the shop rattle and that, together with the hardness of the pavement, made sleep difficult. They suddenly became aware of how vulnerable they were, lying down on the pavement. Sleep came eventually, but not for long. At two in the morning a car full of drunken youths roared past. There were shouts of abuse, and the car disappeared round the corner.

Then it came back again, and the half-asleep clergymen realized they could be in serious trouble. A street fight with a gang of drunks was not what they had planned. As it happened, the car did not stop and there was no trouble. But it was very hard to get back to sleep.

Daylight and the first buses finally came and the sleepers felt a sense of achievement at having stayed out all night. But their satisfaction was short-lived. As people queued at the nearby bus-stop there were unpleasant comments: words like 'Scum' and 'Disgusting'. One of the clergy saw someone he knew and called out, but the man, apparently not recognizing him, looked away and walked off.

It was with a sense of relief that they finally abandoned their cardboard boxes and went their separate ways. All were of one mind: a bath, a well-deserved breakfast and a good sleep in their own beds.

The next night the weather turned bad. It was cold, with lashing rain. Thank goodness they were not out in that. But what about the people who were really homeless? They were still out in it.

Three weeks later, just before Christmas, two of the clergy met by chance. 'Got over the sleep-out?' asked one in a jocular tone.

'Yes, I've been OK this last couple of days,' said the other, 'but before that I couldn't sleep at night. I felt guilty having a bed. I kept looking out of the window at the rain and thinking about the people who were still out there.'

Six months later he had given up his comfortable church ministry and was working alongside homeless people in a nearby city.

What had happened? Seven people made a simple and not very courageous gesture of solidarity with the homeless. They were equipped with all the high-tech thermal clothing they needed. They were tucked up in nice cardboard boxes with a pizza each. And they were woken up the next morning

with cups of tea and bacon sandwiches. The police had been
informed. Their own cars were just yards away round the
corner. Apart from a bit of a scare with the car full of drunks,
it had been a quiet night. It had felt like a bit of a gimmick:
phoney, unreal. Perhaps patronizing?

A simple sleep-out. A few hours on a pavement. Lots of
people do it. But for one of those well-meaning clergy something had happened – and life was never the same again.

What had happened for those three unwise men? What
are they thinking as they slip quietly out of our sight on their
journey home? Time for a bath, breakfast and a good long
sleep? Would they keep in touch with each other? Perhaps
have an annual reunion and try to figure out what it all
meant? They have long since disappeared, and we are left
with our confusion and our unanswered questions – and the
frog child.

But the memory lingers: a great journey, a cattle shed, and
a child. Bacon sandwiches, a battered old cardboard box still
in our cellar, and a few feet of pavement outside the Co-op
which will always be a special place.

28 DECEMBER

Time for change

————◆————

My school career was not a resounding success. At the end of a colourful fifth year our classroom door somehow fell off and I was invited to leave. It was an invitation I couldn't refuse. My best friend Tony Longbottom and I had just four O levels between us.

One of the unexpected highlights of those grim years had been when I came top in Geography, not a complicated subject as long as you remember which way up to hold the map.

And of course we do. The world is straightforward and reassuringly stable. At the top and at the left is America; top right is Russia; and there at the top and in the middle is Britain. Slightly but significantly below us are France and other foreign countries. Much further down the map are places like Africa, India and China. At the bottom are Australia and New Zealand.

King Herod was also good at geography – political geography, anyway. Like most successful politicians, he knew which way up his map was going to be. He was at the top, and that was where he planned to stay. Other people were lower down on the map, and that's where they were going to stay.

That clarity of thought is quite important if you want to control people. First, you need everyone to know where they fit in. Then you need to make sure they stay where they have been put. It also helps if people understand that very unpleasant things will happen if they suddenly get uppity and try to move around the map.

Years ago there was a little rhyme: 'God bless the squire and his relations, and keep us in our proper stations.' Those

101

were the good old days, when you knew where you were. Centuries ago the country was run by the king, with a little help from the Archbishop of Canterbury; women were treated as little more than chattels and the men did all the thinking – and the killing.

The men also made the money and discovered foreign lands. The white man discovered America, Africa and Australia. Despite the fact that the Americans, the Africans and the Australians had been living there quite successfully for several hundred thousand years.

That was long ago, but the mind-set still operates. When people talk about the repatriation of immigrants, they usually mean people leaving predominantly white European countries and returning to their economically weaker countries of ethnic origin. Few people think in terms of the Americans, the Africans and the Australians repatriating their white immigrants back to Europe.

Some things may have moved on, but our social and political geography has not changed very much. We are still at the top. The map is still the right way up. The materially and politically powerful nations are up above and the less powerful and wealthy stay down below.

In the West, no one in their right mind would have a map of the world with Britain and America at the bottom. But why not? Who says that the planet is 'this way up'? Maybe it should be sideways with the North and South Poles at the left- and right-hand sides. But people with power do not like to think of such things.

And that's why Herod's power was threatened by the birth of the little frog. Whether or not Herod was in fact worried, he certainly should have been. Not because this was just another king, but because this one, although he did not know it, was going to turn the map upside down.

The people at the bottom were going to be at the top, and the people at the top would be at the bottom. The hungry would be filled, not with junk food or canned beef from an economic mountain of unwanted produce, but with *good* things. And the rich would be sent away empty; the mighty would be put down from their seats of arrogance and power, and the homeless and the weak would be lifted up.

'The map,' says the Christ person, 'is going to be the other way up. The whistle has gone for half-time and now we change ends. Things are not as you have been given to understand. Things need to change.'

Change? If there is one word that the Church and other vested-interest groups do not like, it is 'change'. The Church does not like change, and when there are changes, they come slowly and painfully. There is a huge emphasis on tradition and a deep suspicion of anything that is new and unfamiliar.

Perhaps that is why, after only a few hundred years, the Church was taken over by the politicians and its bishops started wearing the royal purple.

Ever since the Emperor Constantine made Christianity the official religion of the Roman world in about AD 300 and made church-going a passport to political and social success, there has been an awesome collusion between Church and state. Since that time, the Church has again and again been used as an instrument of economic and political oppression.

Herod was wise to try to crush the little frog, but he missed his target. The vested interests of religion and politics succeeded 30 years later where he had failed. But even then it was not the end of the story. Finally Constantine made it happen. Instead of persecuting the Church as others had done, he privatized it.

How strange that after being beaten with so many sticks, the gospel of the little frog still exists. The Magnificat is lived out by the damaged and dishonoured poor and by a faithful Kingdom remnant within the Church itself.

And the whisper of God's love for the little people is still heard above the roar of the guns and the Christmas cash registers.

Dying and living

————•◆•————

The man sat in the firelight holding the sleeping child. She was only a few days old and had been named Alison. In the silence, he looked down on this small, strange newborn creature. He studied her tiny, perfectly formed fingers; the minute fingernails; the translucent softness of her face and lips; the faint frown which momentarily crossed her sleeping face.

He was enthralled by this small person lying in the crook of his arm. He was far stronger than she was. With one movement he could have crushed the life out of her. But as she lay sleeping, he felt in awe of her. What a journey she had made: through the veil of existence into life here among them. For nine long months she had single-mindedly concentrated on the task of being born. No foolish word had ever crossed her lips, and no idle or unkind thought had ever cheapened her mind.

Even as she slept, she was about the serious work of being alive. It was as though she was a traveller from another world, and he felt humbled by the quiet integrity with which she graced his home. She was the traveller; he was merely the innkeeper. Twenty years later she still frowns and is still a person of great integrity. They have become good friends, but he is still slightly in awe of her.

Did the mother feel that same sense of privilege and awe as she held the Christ-child in the crook of her arm and watched the firelight play on his sleeping face?

Perhaps the Christmas story is so powerful because it touches us at the deepest and most primitive levels of our being. Birth, life, promise, fear and danger are all part of the unfolding drama, and we instinctively relate to that because

the Christ-child's birth is like our birth and Mary's parenthood is like our parenthood. But anyone who runs the risk
of loving soon learns the meaning of vulnerability. Perhaps
from the beginning the mother knew that with this child, her
life would not be easy.

Jewish religious law required a mother to go through a
ceremony of purification 40 days after the birth of a male
child. Childbirth was a great blessing but it was, in those
days, thought to be unclean. It was therefore necessary for a
ritual act of cleansing to take place. This is significant for us
for three reasons.

First, it shows one of the early links between sex and sin.
For centuries biblical texts have been used selectively and
often out of context to condemn sex as sinful, unclean, and
to be disapproved of in almost all situations.

Second, the fact that the mother of the Christ-child took
part in this ceremony suggests that either she was doing so
under social and family pressure, or that she believed that it
was an appropriate action. Appropriate if the child was
conceived by the Holy Spirit of God and not by a human
father? Was the birth of the Son of God inherently unclean
and sinful? Or was the Christ-child's birth not regarded in
such an exalted way at that moment?

Third, the ceremony is significant because of what appears
to have happened during their visit to the Temple. According
to Luke, there was a man there called Simeon who was a
wise and holy person. Simeon believed he would not die
before he had seen with his own eyes the Messiah, the deliverer, the promised one of God.

When the Christ-child was brought into the Temple, says
Luke, Simeon knew that moment had come. 'Now you can
let me die, Lord,' he says. 'I have seen your promise fulfilled.
This is the one who will bring meaning into the world, for
Gentile as well as for Jew.'

But, Luke tells us, there is sorrow here as well as joy.
Simeon turns to the mother and says: 'This child will bring
life and hope to many people, but he will also provoke
opposition and hatred. And you, too, because you love him,

will be caught up in that conflict. Your own heart will be pierced with pain.'

Suddenly the whole Christ event opens up before us. The child is less than six weeks old and already his death is in sight. Why? Why should this be? And why was it so obvious to Simeon on that day?

Because action and reaction are equal and opposite. And what is true in physics often seems to be true in human relationships. There is a perverse tendency to rubbish what is wholesome; to spoil what is beautiful; to condemn people who try to help others as 'do-gooders' and to be envious of other people's good fortune and achievements. And, sometimes, to oppose love with hatred.

What was it that evoked such opposition and hatred among those in positions of power to this apparently insignificant Christ person? Above all else it seems to have been the lack of boundaries. He did not respond to normal cataloguing; the labels would not stick. One minute he was an itinerant preacher, easy to categorize, but the next minute they had lost him. They could not identify or control him.

One example among many in the short life of Jesus encapsulates this dilemma. And ironically it begins with a mother experiencing the agonizing pain that Simeon foretold for Mary that day in the Temple.

It is 30 years later. Jesus is walking down the road to a town called Nain with a large crowd of followers. Suddenly coming towards them from the town is a funeral procession.

Sensibly, the Christ person might have turned aside in respect to allow the funeral procession to pass by, and to avoid being defiled by coming into contact with this death. But he does not turn away. To everyone's horror, he actually halts the funeral procession and speaks to the woman who has been bereaved.

Suddenly we are out of control. But watch what happens next.

The woman is a widow and the dead person is her only son. First she has been widowed but, as if that were not enough, disaster has struck again with the death of her beloved child. The sword of death has twice entered her heart. For her it is the end of the world. She is like the walking dead as she follows his open coffin to the grave.

But instead of expressing quiet words of sympathy with the widow, Jesus' reaction is one of anger. Anger and a deep compassion at the overwhelming pain of the situation. And in the next moment he does two startling things.

First he touches the open coffin. That may seem to us a simple gesture of human concern, but in that instant he is ritually defiled. In that moment he has crossed a forbidden line to share in both the pain – and the defilement – of the widow. In an action which reminds us of the healing of the leper in the opening pages of Mark's gospel, Jesus is touched by the overwhelming pain of the situation. And he reacts by engaging with that pain. He reveals his immediate and unconditional solidarity with the outcast and the unclean by touching them in a simple but profound gesture of human love.

Then, Luke tells us, the Christ person speaks to the dead child – and the young boy is in some way brought back to life. And the people shout out in amazement: 'God has visited his people!'

God has visited his people in this man? But if this person is in any way the human expression of God, what sort of God are we talking about? Not a God who says childbirth is unclean, but a God who hugs lepers and reaches out in fierce and powerful compassion to touch the dead.

Yes, King Herod was wise to try to kill this little frog. Even in this short story the labels do not stay attached. The map has been turned upside down, and God exalted above the heavens is suddenly here in the gutter with the grieving and the dead.

The crowd are right: God is here. With a grieving mother in Palestine and a grieving mother in South Africa; with a little boy standing beside a newspaper-seller in the dark streets of the city and with a homeless man shouting out his despair and emptiness.

But vested interests do not want that sort of love, or maps

turned upside down. They do not want an uncontrollable and unpredictable God. They want quiet and ordered religion and a map which stays where they put it: with them at the top. And so the little frog must die.

Suddenly the womb and the tomb seem very close. Life and death are never very far apart in this Christ event. Four days past the festivities of Christmas and already we can see a hill with three crosses on it. The widow's son lived, the leper was healed and all received new life.

But the Christ-child who bears those gifts will have to die.

30 DECEMBER

Innocent victims

---◆---

One of my most treasured possessions is a small wooden cross. It was given to me when I went on a retreat in Ely. It's called a bog oak cross and the wood is about 5,000 years old. The story of the bog oak cross is fascinating.

Thousands of years ago there were lots of trees in the flat fenlands of East Anglia. Whether it was the end of the Ice Age or not, I can't remember, but for some reason the whole area was suddenly flooded.

The trees died and gradually collapsed into the deep water. Over the centuries their trunks were buried under the silt. The softer woods rotted, but the oak became pickled in the sea water that had flooded the region.

For thousands of years – long before the birth of Christ – their timber lay buried under the sea bed. The centuries passed and Christianity came to England. The great cathedral of Ely was built on an island. Then, years later, the surrounding land was drained and became good farmland. Generations of honest ploughing disturbed the soil and gradually the wood of the great oak trees came to the surface.

Some of that ancient wood, which lived 3,000 years before the birth of Christ, was taken and shaped into the dark wooden cross on my desk today. It is only a small thing, but it never ceases to amaze me that something which had been dead for so long could be lifted up and fashioned into a symbol of life.

It makes me think back to the Christ person and the way in which he died and was buried, and yet was somehow raised up as sign of life. It makes me think of my friends on the streets and in the bed and breakfast places and of the Magnificat promise, that somehow they will be raised up as a sign of life.

For me they are that already, but what about the other poor: those so poor that their lives will end today?

A few days after the Dunblane massacre, in which a gunman burst into a primary school and shot dead a number of defenceless children, a headline appeared in a magazine. It read: 'The day 4,016 children died'. It looked back on the day of the massacre in that Scottish school. Without diminishing in any way the tragedy and horror of that event, it asked people to think of the other 4,000 children who were also killed that day.

Why do we not remember them? Perhaps because they were foreign children. Each and every day, says the United Nations, they die in their thousands because of the marketing policies of some of the world's largest food companies. Companies whose names are on every supermarket shelf and on goods in our own kitchen cupboards. Companies who make baby milk.

And it is the baby milk, that sign of nourishment and hope for the newborn, that is the problem. In order to increase profits, some unthinking food companies push sales of powdered baby food in Third World countries. A packet of baby milk can cost a week's wages for a family, but the mothers are persuaded that artificial baby food is better than breast milk. And, to encourage its use, free samples are given away. Once customers are hooked on the product, the free samples stop.

In order to make the artificial baby milk go further, the mothers dilute the powder, which then becomes less nutritious. It is diluted with water, which is often polluted. The mothers' breast milk dries up. The babies become undernourished and often ill. And 4,000 of them die each day. The bringer of food becomes the bringer of death.

But these people are on the other side of the world. They are invisible and expendable. The food companies maximize profits so that their shareholders will benefit. Who are the shareholders? Pension funds and unit trusts, in which we prudently invest our money.

Between Christmas and New Year the Church has a festival called the Slaughter of the Innocents. It marks the day when King Herod, in an attempt to kill the Christ-child, had all the children under the age of two years in the town of Bethlehem killed. But his attempt failed. The Christ-child and his parents had fled, becoming refugees in a foreign country, says St Matthew.

Between Christmas and New Year, we reflect on the story of the Christ-child. After days of eating and drinking, perhaps we should sit quietly for a few moments with a cup of tea and think what it all means, and reflect on the children whose deaths we will help to bring about today.

Will it be a massacre? A Dunblane? No, it will be silent and it will pass unnoticed. But is it really any better for a child to die of malnutrition in its mother's arms than for it to be put to the sword or killed by a madman with a gun? We would never use a gun or strike with a sword, and yet we play our part in those 4,000 infant deaths each day.

Maybe in the coming year we need to have the courage to begin to change the map, so that the people at the bottom come a bit nearer the top and are recognized to be human beings. And so that we become a bit more human, too.

31 DECEMBER

Tell me why

It's strange how it's always the simple questions that are the hardest to answer. After 40 years of gardening, I suddenly want to ask: why do things grow? I know about photosynthesis and the effect of the sun on plants, but so what? Why should moisture and warmth and sunlight make anything grow?

Why does a seed in the dark, wet earth suddenly decide to turn into a plant? Why bother? Couldn't it just stay put and do nothing? What makes it push and struggle through the earth into the open air? And, equally amazing, what makes it want to push its delicate roots down into the earth with all those hard stones getting in the way?

At the age of seven, my daughter Lindsey suddenly asked: 'What is life for?' I didn't have an answer then and I'm not sure I've discovered one since. Unless it is that life isn't a static 'thing' existing in isolation, but is more like a process. Perhaps we should be asking: why does life happen?

Why do most of us get out of bed in the morning? Probably because there are things we want to do – or have to do. Situations into which we feel drawn. Bed always feels more comfortable, so why get up? It's the same with the seed. Hidden away in the ground it probably feels quite safe. But, stick your head up above ground, and a lot of unpleasant things can happen. You may get trodden on or eaten, or someone may come along with a lawnmower. Growth involves risk and, for us, growth requires courage.

It's as though we have a choice. We can either stay indoors with the curtains drawn shut and the television on and hide, or we can open the front door and risk going outside. As we

112

have seen before, there has been a great temptation for religion to provide a sort of safe haven where people can hide from life. And, in truth, there are times when people who are tired or injured need a time and a place of shelter to recover.

But providing a safe haven is not the primary reason for faith, and it is not the reality we see lived out in the gospels or, come to think of it, in our Advent adventure.

Looking back, there is a seemingly minor event which happens three times in the opening pages of Luke. Together these three events constitute a simple but profound discovery about God and about life. And they all involve the experience of fear.

First, the barren woman, Elizabeth, conceives in her old age, but when her husband hears the news from the angel, what does he experience? Not elation but a fear that overcomes him. He is no longer in control; he is suddenly out of his depth and vulnerable. Was it real fear? Was it significant fear? And, if not, why did Luke bother to mention it? 'Do not be afraid,' the angel says to him.

A few verses later it happens again. This time the uneducated and undeserving Mary is told that she will conceive and bear the Christ-child. The lowly peasant girl's immediate reaction, as we have seen, is also one of fear. Again the angels speaks the words of reassurance: 'Do not be afraid.'

Third, there is the account of the unclean and undeserving shepherds on the hillside. When the angel appears to them to tell them of the birth of the Christ-child they are not just afraid, they are terror-stricken, says Luke. But again there come the same words: 'Do not be afraid.'

To each group of people – the barren and powerless; the humble and lowly; and the unclean and outcast – a great gift is given. Together they represent three huge sections of humanity. To each in turn the undeserved gift of life is proclaimed and given. Each in turn is drawn into the dynamic and unfolding drama of God's creation. And each feels overwhelming fear. Fear of the unknown; fear of the awesome presence of God; fear of that which they cannot control.

But these are not isolated incidents which happen only in

the prologue to Luke's gospel. When we listen again to those three 'Do not be afraid' passages, a further thought comes to mind. Where else have we heard those words?

Suddenly we realize that we hear these words at crisis moments of particular significance when God reveals something dramatically new about life – and about the Christ person.

Remember Peter's words at the moment he realizes who Jesus is. They have fished all night without success, but Jesus tells them to let down their nets once again. Peter at first argues, but then agrees. The result is a huge catch. But what does Peter do? He doesn't say 'Thank you' but falls at the feet of the Christ person in fear and says: 'Go away from me.' But now it is Jesus who speaks the words of reassurance: 'Do not be afraid.'

It happens again in that strange but important incident on the mountain-top when Jesus is revealed in glory as the Christ person. The disciples at first want to set up camp and to prolong the experience, but suddenly they are overshadowed by the presence of God and they are afraid.

Finally, it happens after the Crucifixion, when a group of courageous women go to the tomb to clean and lay out Jesus' body. But, instead of a dead body, they find life. Again, the reaction is not one of immediate happiness and celebration – it is one of terror. But again there come the words of reassurance.

At each point life takes a huge leap forward, and at each point there is the same sequence of events: the discovery or revelation of something new and unexpected; a sense of fear and uncertainty; and almost always the words of reassurance.

The scriptures are the story of the gift of life from God. Again and again women and men are led forward by something outside themselves into new discoveries and new realizations of what life is about. Each step brings the uncertainty of growth and the fear of the unknown. But at each step they are met with the same reassurance: 'Do not be afraid.'

As we prepare to step across the threshold of the new year, we ask ourselves: what is life about? If we choose, it can be nothing more than a hiding away from reality and discomfort. But if we have the courage to engage with the Advent adventure, we may discover its real meaning.

But it will not be without its risks: to our finances as we reflect on the way our investments are used; to our politics, as we remember that the way we vote often reflects the way we love our neighbour; and to our faith itself, as we realize that true faith is not a matter of security and certainty, but of risk and change. If we follow that course of action we will need to hear in our own lives those words: 'Do not be afraid.'

1 JANUARY

Dare we say yes?

————◆————

Ask anyone how many words there are in the Lord's Prayer and they'll get it wrong. Fifty? A hundred? The clever ones might say it depends which translation you mean. Wrong again. The answer is: one. The whole of the Lord's Prayer, and the whole of the Christian faith, is summed up in that one word. And the word is: 'Abba'.

Jesus spoke a language called Aramaic and the Lord's Prayer begins with the one Aramaic word: Abba. We have traditionally translated it as 'Father', but the word actually means 'Daddy'. It is the word a child uses in the familiarity of the home when speaking to a parent. It is not a childish or trivial word, but one which implies warmth, trust and love. It is a word of intimacy and affection, as well as a recognition of power and authority.

Because of the intimate and child-like nature of the word, people over the years have preferred the more dignified expression 'Our Father'. But, in substituting their word for the Jesus word, they have significantly changed and obscured what the Christ person was saying. Once again, he was not religious enough or dignified enough for them.

And so it is that day in and day out Christians say the Lord's Prayer, often with hardly a thought about its revolutionary meaning. 'Our Father', we begin, and then barrel through the rest of the words which are so familiar that we can actually say them while thinking about other things. Which is probably just as well – unless we want to get caught up in a revolution.

There seems little doubt that when Jesus taught his followers to pray and told them to say that first word, Abba, he knew what a shocking thing he was doing. Before that, no one had dared to address God in such a way. God was all-powerful, distant, and impersonal. But Abba is just the opposite: close, familiar, warm, intimate and even vulnerable. Abba is the word for the male parent, but carries with it many of the connotations of the mother.

But if Abba shocked the people listening to Jesus, it doesn't shock us. Not at first, anyway. Praying the Lord's Prayer is a bit like going swimming. You think you are stepping into the shallow end, but suddenly find the water is over your head. And with the Lord's Prayer it all happens with the first word.

If we speak the word 'Abba', and believe what we say, we are instantly out of our depth. It means that the almighty and everlasting God, whose name is hallowed, loves each of us personally in the sacrament of this present moment with the intimacy of a strong and loving mother and a good and loving father. It means there are no barriers with God.

The problem is that it means there are no barriers at all. It means that the whole of our Advent adventure has been happening within that gentle, courteous and over-arching love. That the homeless people we have met and the threadbare, middle-aged priest are also held within that over-arching love. For this God is Abba to them too. It means that the politicians and bishops we have grumbled about are also precious to this Abba.

The Lord's Prayer is dangerous and revolutionary because in its first word it demolishes the barriers between all of us: the rich and the poor; the housed and the homeless; the clothed and the naked; the hungry and the well fed. We say 'give us today our daily bread.' But who is the 'us' we are talking about? Me and my family or me and the Abba family, the whole of humankind?

It was St Basil the Great who said that the clothes belong to the naked and the food belongs to the hungry. And someone else, not so great, said that all property was theft. And in the context of today's world, were they so very wrong?

If the clothes belong to the naked, then what right have I to have two coats when my friends in this city have none? How can I complain about the queues at the supermarket checkout when 4,000 children may be needlessly dying every day, every one of them just as precious to the Abba of the Christ person as I am?

This one small word blows apart the idea that prayer is a religious activity disconnected from life. I pray as I live. But if I do not live as I pray, my prayer is a lie.

Why is this? Because prayer is a response to the unconditional love of God. Prayer is part of that love. But love is a social activity that happens in the real world. We cannot distinguish between prayer and action. Prayer is part of the action.

If that's the case, then maybe it's better to forget this Abba prayer and stay in shallow water. But how can we set aside the Abba prayer when this is the prayer of Jesus himself? How can we be Christians and not say the prayer of the Christ person?

But if we live our lives in his Abba prayer and ground our faith in the love that he lived out among the poor and the outcast, we are in for a rough ride. And he himself warns us how rough it can get. 'Will you take up your own cross and follow me?' he asks. 'Would you be willing to die for me?' Christianity is a rough faith. There are splinters and nails, and some of the time it's not very sweet-smelling.

And it's all there in our Advent story. The angels who are there at the birth are there at the tomb when it is time for the death. The outcast and unclean shepherds become the first evangelists bringing the good news to the mother of the Christ-child, and the priesthood of this new dispensation is the priesthood of the poor.

The fear of the coming labour echoes the fear of Gethsemane and the labour of the coming death. The fear at the first understanding of the birth is echoed by the fear at the first understanding of resurrection. The Christ-child of the mother in the stable is the Christ-child of God nailed to the Cross.

As we come to this new year we have a choice. Looking down the months and years, with the rest of our lives stretching out before us, a voice says: 'I am with you. Do not be afraid.'

But dare we take the risk and say: 'Abba'?